Home Banking with Quicken

Steve Cummings

MIS:
PRESS

A Subsidiary of
Henry Holt and Co., Inc.

First Edition—1996

Printed in the United States of America.

```
Cummings, Steve.
  Home banking with Quicken / by Steve Cummings.
      p.  cm.
  ISBN 1-55828-477-X
  1. Home banking services. 2. Quicken for Windows. 3. Finance,
Personal--Computer programs.  I. Title
HG171.C86    1996
332.024'0028'5369--dc20                                    95-50763
                                                               CIP
```

10 9 8 7 6 5 4 3 2 1

MIS:Press books are available at special discounts for bulk purchases for sales promotions, premiums, fund-raising, or educational use. Special editions or book excerpts can also be created to specification.

For details contact: Special Sales Director
                          MIS:Press
                          a subsidiary of Henry Holt and Company, Inc.
                          115 West 18th Street
                          New York, New York 10011

Associate Publisher: Paul Farrell	**Managing Editor:** Cary Sullivan
Development Editor: Judy Brief	**Copy Editor:** Judy Brief

Technical Editor: Rick Jaroslovsky

Production Editor: Anthony Washington

Contents

iv

V

viii

ix

Introduction

Home Banking with Quicken is your practical guide to today's cresting revolution in online money management. With this book, you can take immediate advantage of all the benefits offered by the marriage of personal computer technology with the banking world.

My main objective is to help you accomplish your banking and money management chores as quickly and painlessly as possible. Whether you're new to computers or an old hand with Quicken itself, this book will show you when and how to use the financial services available online (over the telephone lines) via your computer. The accent is on your bottom line, rather than on the technical aspects of working with your computer.

On the other hand, you need a tool for every job. For the foreseeable future, Quicken is going to be the right tool for home banking. That's why this book amply covers Quicken basics as well as all the features you'll need for efficient home banking. But look elsewhere if you want an exhaustive reference to Quicken. (Then again, don't rush to buy one—Quicken is an easy program to use and it bends over backwards to help you learn its operations.)

This book assumes you already have some basic understanding of how to run Windows and Windows applications. For example, you should know how to start programs, how to switch between running programs, and how to make choices from Windows menus and dialog boxes. You should know, for example, how to double-click with the mouse (click twice in quick succession), and how to switch between the panels of a "tabbed" dialog box (at the top of the box, you click on the "notebook tab" for the panel you want). You should also know how to pick options from a *drop-down list* (which appears when you click the arrow button to the right of many dialog box fill-in items, or fields). Even if you haven't yet fully mastered these skills, though, you should be able to manage the material presented here—I've made a conscious effort to avoid jargon and spell out the steps required for each task in point-by-point instructions.

If you've used previous versions of Quicken, you may still want to consider this book as a guide to the full-scale home banking features now included. Compared to the Quicken manual, this book provides far more extensive coverage of online features, especially when it comes to putting them to best use in real-world financial management. Quicken 5 (for 96) has lots of new features not directly related to home banking, and I summarize many of these as well.

The plan of this book is simple. Chapter 1 introduces home banking, reviewing the range of financial transactions you can conduct from your computer, as well as the advantages and possible pitfalls they present. In Chapter 2, you learn to get Quicken running on your system and how to prepare for home banking. The next few chapters cover basic Quicken skills such as recording transactions and paying bills, as well as automating and customizing your records. With these under your belt, you go on to learn ways you can put online financial services and Quicken to work to simplify money management headaches and build your net worth.

CHAPTER ONE:

Why Home Banking?

Like the ATM (Automatic Teller Machines) revolution did in the late 1970s, banking from home by computer—"branchless banking"—is bound to transform the way we manage our everyday financial affairs. No one has yet figured out a way to send cash over the telephone wire, but you can carry out almost every other kind of financial transaction from home—if you have a computer and the right software.

Likely as not, that software will be Quicken. For years, Quicken has been the most popular software for managing personal finances. With the introduction of Quicken 5 for Windows (and a comparable version for the Macintosh), Quicken turns your home computer into a full-fledged banking machine.

The Technology of Home Banking

How does Quicken do it? If you've somehow escaped contact with computer-based communications, you deserve a gentle (and brief) introduction to the technology of home banking. Here goes: Two computers at different locations can transfer information back and forth over ordinary telephone lines. To do this, they rely on devices called *modems*.

The modem connected to one computer converts information stored in that machine into a form that can travel over telephone lines—if you listen in on the line, you'll hear a raucous noise. At the other end of the line, the second modem unscrambles the noise, turning it back into information the second computer can understand.

Because it relies on a connection via the telephone line, this type of information transfer between computers is often called *online* communications. You can go online—by connecting to the Internet, or to an online information service such as CompuServe—to exchange mail with your friends, buy airline tickets or stereo systems from an online merchant, or look up facts and figures about the world economy or your favorite baseball team.

And with Quicken, you can do your banking online. You'll see how that works a little later in this chapter.

4

What's So Great about Home Banking?

Home banking won't solve the world's great problems and though fun it's not that exciting or entertaining. If your expectations are reasonable, however, you'll find some genuinely positive things about being able to manage your financial dealings from home.

Some of the advantages of home banking are obvious:

- It saves you time. There's no drive to the bank and no line to wait in once you're there.
- It gives you more flexibility. You can conduct your banking business when it suits your schedule, rather than according to the bank's hours.
- It saves gasoline and wear and tear on your car.

For most people, these simple benefits would be reason enough to consider changing their banking habits. But with Quicken, home banking also gives you a leg up on your financial recordkeeping chores, and it can save you money and even help you make a little more.

With home banking via Quicken, keeping track of your financial transactions is quicker and easier than on paper. You end up with more complete, more accurate records as well.

In a moment, we'll look in more detail at the specific services that are available. But let's pause a moment to examine some potential negatives of home banking.

How Much Does Home Banking Cost?

Each bank or financial institution sets its prices for online banking services independently. The fees are typically quite low, on the order of $5 per month each for online banking and online bill payment. The online bill payment service offered by Intuit, Quicken's publisher, currently costs $4.95 per month for 20 payments.

5

What's the Downside?

This may come as a letdown, but Quicken won't do all your work for you. To realize all the benefits of home banking, you have to use it consistently. Yes, record-keeping with Quicken really is *easier* than with pencil and paper. Still, people who don't bother recording their checks or balancing their checkbooks on paper may still find excuses to avoid these chores even when they can be done electronically.

It certainly makes sense to raise questions about the security of your money and financial records with home banking. Transmitting records electronically to a faceless computer at an unknown destination doesn't inspire instant trust. True, your bank will be using security techniques like the ones that safeguard ATM access to ensure that you alone have access to your funds. Still, most people feel a little safer with deposit receipts from a living teller and canceled checks.

It's hard to count the cost of cultural change, but it's clear that there are some losses to consider in the switch away from face-to-face banking. If you make deposits and withdrawals at the ATM and transact all your other business by computer, you may never need to set foot inside the bank again. By giving up contact with the people at the bank, you lose a source of advice and support. You're also much less likely to get a loan based on your good character when the numbers don't quite justify the risk.

Of course, existing technological and economic trends—ATMs and the disappearance of locally-owned banks, for example—have already drastically altered the role of banks as centers of community life. Clearly, however, home banking will make banking a still more impersonal affair.

The Range of Online Financial Services

Even though you can't make deposits or withdrawals with your computer, there are plenty of other banking services available to you with Quicken. Here's a survey of what you can do online:

6

Obtain your current account balance. When you need to know for sure how much money you have available, you can have the answer in a few moments using Quicken.

Get a list of cleared checks. If you're not sure whether that mortgage check you wrote at the last minute has cleared your account yet, ask for a statement of your most recent checks. Working from this list, you can see in a flash whether or not the bank's current balance reflects the checks you've already written.

Transfer funds between accounts. When you have a cash surplus in your checking account, it's always smart to shift the excess to a savings or money market account paying a higher interest rate. Or, when you need to cover a check for an unexpected expense, you can move the necessary funds in the opposite direction. With Quicken and an online account you can move funds back and forth between accounts as often as you need to, without the hassle of driving down to the bank.

Pay your bills. This is a big one. Tell Quicken who you want to pay and how much, and the program does the rest, sending funds to the recipient for you (you'll see how the process works in a bit). No more licking stamps and licking envelopes, no more writer's cramp from all those signatures. Of course, the bank will charge you for this service—but each electronic "check" costs only about as much as a postage stamp, making it considerably less expensive than the comparable paper check. What's more, you can pay all your monthly bills at one sitting, but date them so the funds leave your account at just the right time. Not only is this convenient, your money earns interest longer. And finally, with online bill payment, you can take advantage of all of Quicken's features for automating your bill paying to make preparing your payments each month a breeze (see Chapter 4).

Balance your checkbook records against a monthly electronic bank statement. Your bank statement arrives over the telephone line, complete with transactions such as handwritten checks that you would otherwise have to record in Quicken manually. Then Quicken automates the reconciling process, cutting the time required and minimizing mistakes as it compares the statement against your records.

7

Communicate instantly in writing with the bank's customer service department via e-mail, or "electronic mail." If you have a question, special request, or complaint, you can type it up and send it to the bank using Quicken. The next time you connect with your bank, the reply should be ready for you to read. If your problem doesn't need immediate action, this method can communicate the message more accurately than a phone call, since you get to compose the message ahead of time. It also lets you avoid the nuisance of waiting on hold for "the next available customer service representative." And sending a message like this is *free*—it doesn't even cost you a postage stamp. Of course, you'll still able to call the bank and talk to a human being if you need to.

Retrieve your monthly credit card statement. Once the statement is received, Quicken reconciles it against your own records, then pays the bill automatically if you give the OK.

Obtain up-to-the-minute stock prices. You can use online access to financial market data to track the performance of all your securities—or of investments you're considering—recording the prices in your Quicken records automatically.

NOTE

At the moment, you can't buy or sell securities such as stocks, mutual funds, or bonds online—at least not with Quicken. That's likely to change shortly.

Obtain financial information via the Internet. Quicken comes with the software you need to connect to the Quicken Financial Network, a special area on the Internet's World Wide Web. The Quicken Financial Network offers current mutual fund performance information, seasonal financial advice, and tips and news about Quicken itself.

How Home Banking Works

Before you can begin banking at home, you must first sign up both with your bank and with Intuit, Quicken's publisher. When you sign up, you receive a special identifying number and choose the password that ensures that you alone have access to your money.

NOTE

Quicken treats online bill payment and banking (other banking functions) as separate services. When you sign up, be sure to tell your financial institution whether you want one or both of these services. Some institutions may charge a separate fee for each.

In Quicken, you write the electronic "checks" for these payments on a screen that looks just like a real checkbook. Quicken takes over when you tell it to send the payments, instructing your modem to dial the Intuit service center. This is a centralized computer center through which all online Quicken transactions pass, no matter which institution you bank with. (Intuit doesn't charge you directly for use of the service center, though it does charge the participating financial institutions.)

Before sending the payment instructions, Quicken must verify that you are authorized to access the funds in the account, which it does by sending in your identification number and password. When the service center is satisfied that you have rights to the money, Quicken transmits the payments. In turn, the payment requests are transferred to your bank.

At this point, one of two things happens: If the recipient of the payment is set up to receive funds electronically, your bank transfers the money directly to the recipient's account. For other recipients, the bank simply prints and mails a paper check.

The sequence is similar when you want to balance your checkbook or access other information about your account. After verifying your identifying information, the Intuit service center relays your request to your bank. The bank digs into its files, returning its latest data to Quicken via the service center.

Summary

That's it for this quick tour of home banking theory. From now on we get practical, focusing first on the mechanics of working with Quicken, then building on those skills to make the most of online financial services.

CHAPTER TWO:

Getting Started with Home Banking

Now that you have the big picture on home banking, it's time to get down to business. To get started, you need a copy of Quicken 5 (for 96), a PC capable of running it, and a standard, "Hayes-compatible" modem installed in or attached to the computer. Don't worry if you're not comfortable with computer jargon—just go to a reputable computer dealer who sells Quicken 5 and ask them to set you up with the necessary equipment.

If you can stand a little jargon, here's what your system needs to run Quicken comfortably:

- Windows 3.1, Windows for Workgroups 3.11, or Windows 95. Quicken 5 works fine with Windows 95, but it doesn't take advantage of Windows 95's new features such as long file names.

- An IBM-compatible PC. If you're running Windows 3.1 or Windows for Workgroups, a 386 processor and 4 megabytes of memory (RAM) are quite adequate. If you have Windows 95, or if you're running the CD-ROM version of Quicken, you should have a 486 processor and at least 8 megabytes of RAM.

- The amount of free hard disk space you need varies depending on which Quicken version you're installing, but 25 megabytes is enough for any version.

- A standard VGA monitor and graphics board (16 colors and 640 by 480 resolution) will do fine for running Quicken itself, including the online banking features. However, you need a 256-color display to run the extra multimedia programs that come with Quicken Deluxe. A higher-resolution screen lets you see more information at a glance.

- A Hayes-compatible modem. An inexpensive 2400 bits-per-second (bps) modem is adequate for electronically managing your bank accounts, paying your bills, and getting your credit card statements. If you want to access the Quicken Financial Network on the Internet, your modem speed should be at least 9600 bps, and 14,400 bps (14.4) or 28,800 bps (28.8) modems are preferable.

- To use the multimedia features of the CD-ROM version of Quicken, you need a double-speed CD-ROM drive (of course) and a MPC 2-compatible sound card with speakers.

- A Windows-compatible printer for printing reports and graphs.

Installing Quicken

Before you do anything else you have to install Quicken, transferring the software to your hard disk where the computer can run it. Quicken comes with a guide to setting up the program on your computer, but here's a quick summary of the steps:

1. Start Windows if you haven't already done so.

2. If you're installing from floppy disks (diskettes), make backup copies of all the disks and put them away in a safe place. Use the techniques for copying disks described in your Windows manual.

3. Put the first Quicken disk into a floppy disk drive, or insert the Quicken CD-ROM in your CD-ROM player.

4. To begin the actual installation, activate the RUN command found on the Start menu in Windows 95, or on the File menu in the Windows 3.1 Program Manager.

5. From the RUN command's dialog box, click **Browse**, switch to the drive with the installation disk, and locate the Setup.exe program in the list of files.

6. Double-click on Setup.exe to start it.

7. If you're installing a version of Quicken that comes with add-on programs such as Quicken Home Inventory, Setup presents a list of these components and lets you pick out which to install.

8. Setup noses around in your system to determine whether you have enough hard disk space for the Quicken files, and suggests the drive and directory where it plans to install Quicken. Make any changes you wish, and then choose **OK** to go ahead with the installation.

9. Setup copies Quicken to your hard disk. If you're installing from diskettes you'll be notified when to insert each disk.

NOTE

If you're upgrading from an earlier version of Quicken you'll already have at least one Quicken file containing your financial records. The installation process locates old Quicken files and gives you the opportunity to convert them for use with Quicken 5.

10. When Setup has completed its work, store the original Quicken master disks or the CD-ROM in a safe place.

Setting up Your Quicken Records

Grab your most recent bank statement for your checking account and go to work.

Running Quicken the First Time

Once Quicken is installed, running it is easy. In Windows 95, click the **Start** button, then choose **Programs** —> **Quicken** —> **Quicken 5 for Windows**. In Windows 3.1, find the Quicken group in Program Manager and double-click on the **Quicken 5** icon.

Each time you start Quicken you'll see a preliminary welcome screen as Quicken gets ready for action. After that, the very first time you run the program, the New User Setup window (Figure 2.1) gently coaxes you into jumping right in with Quicken.

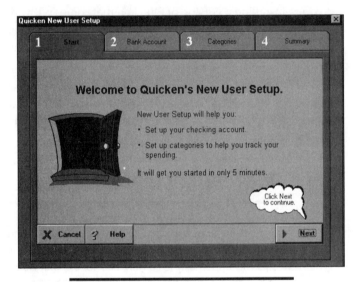

Figure 2.1 The New User Setup window.

NOTE

If you've just upgraded from a previous version of Quicken, you won't see New User Setup when you start Quicken. Instead, you'll be offered a chance to see a help window listing new features and other changes in Quicken 5.

Here's the idea: Before you can do any work with Quicken, you need a place to store the financial information you'll soon be poring over. So, when you run it for the first time, Quicken makes sure that you set up the electronic filing system you'll need.

About Quicken Accounts and Files

Quicken organizes your electronic records into *accounts* that correspond to the checking, savings, and credit card accounts you already have with your bank and other financial institutions. To record even a single financial transaction, you need at least one Quicken account.

You can have up to 255 separate accounts in a single Quicken *file*. Like all Windows applications, Quicken uses files stored on disk as the units of storage for related information. But you won't need to pay much attention to your Quicken files—one Quicken file is enough for most people. And unlike many other programs, Quicken takes care of saving and opening your file automatically.

NOTE

If you've upgraded from a previous version of Quicken, and assuming your existing files were located during the installation of Quicken 5, you won't have to set up any accounts from scratch. Skip to the section "The Main Quicken Window and HomeBase," later in this chapter.

15

Setting up Your First Account

You'll learn more about how Quicken accounts and files work later. For now, let the series of panels in New User Setup walk you through the process of setting up your first Quicken account: one that mirrors your main, real-life checking account.

All you have to do is read some basic information and answer a few easy questions. After you've finished with each "page" of the New User Setup sequence, click on the button labeled **Next** at the bottom right of the window to move to the following panel. The "tabs" at the top of the New User Setup window (labeled *Start, Bank Account,* and so forth) tell you which part of the setup process you're working on at the moment. Behind the scenes, Quicken sets up your first file as well.

Follow these steps to start your first account:

1. Click the **Next** button to move to the first "action" panel, shown in Figure 2.2. All you do here is type in a name for your checking account. You can name the account anything you like, but you're limited to 15 characters (letters, numerals, and punctuation marks).

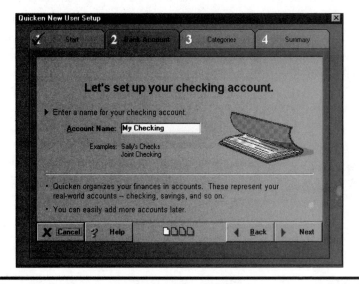

Figure 2.2 Enter a name for your new checking account in this panel.

2. Click **Next** again. Quicken asks you whether you have a bank statement to work from. Click over the **Yes** or **No** button as appropriate.

3. If you're working from a bank statement, Quicken asks you to enter two basic pieces of information about the statement: its ending date and the ending balance (that is, the last date covered by the statement, and the final balance in your account on that date). See Figure 2.3.

   You can type in the date, using the month/day/year format, but it's easier to use Quicken's pop-up date entry calendar, shown here:

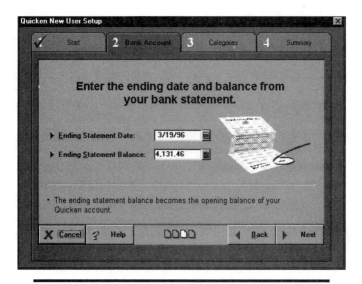

Figure 2.3 Enter information about the bank statement you're working with in this panel.

Click the little blue icon (picture) beside the date area to display the calendar. Select the month using the arrows at the top, then click on the date to finish the entry and close the pop-up calendar.

4. Type in the statement balance in the space provided. You can also enter the balance using the pop-up calculator, as shown here:

This little calculator lets you enter numerals by clicking (though doing so usually takes longer than typing them in). If you do want to use the pop-up calculator, display it by clicking the little icon to the right of the balance area. Click the button labeled **Enter** to finalize your entry.

5. Clicking **Next** at this point begins a short course in *categories*, Quicken's system for classifying income and expense items into groups. Examples include "Interest Income" and "Groceries." The next two or three panels provide basic information about categories. For now, this summary will do—we'll look at categories in more detail in Chapter 3.

6. A few clicks on the **Next** button brings you to the panel shown in Figure 2.4. Here, your job is to decide whether you want only home-related categories in your account, or business-related categories as well. Click on the appropriate statement.

The choice you make here applies to all accounts in this file.

NOTE

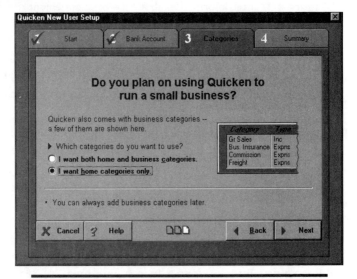

Figure 2.4 Use this panel to select which set of built-in categories you want to use with your Quicken file.

7. That brings you to the Summary panel shown in Figure 2.5. Quicken shows you all the information you've just entered in

one place, allowing you to review it and make any necessary changes.

Figure 2.5 This panel summarizes the information you've entered for your new account.

8. A final click on the **Next** button completes the account setup process. Note that Quicken hasn't asked you anything yet about online banking, even though you won't be able to use it until you turn it on, figuratively speaking. That step comes later.

After Setting up Your First Account...

The last panel on the New User Setup window lays out your next two options: You can click **Done** to go directly to Quicken proper, or you can click the **QuickTours** button. The latter choice lets you access a simple yet comprehensive overview of Quicken's features, introducing the skills you'll need to use them.

Figure 2.6 shows the opening window for QuickTours. When you finish using QuickTours, click **Done** or **Use Quicken** to go on to the main Quicken display.

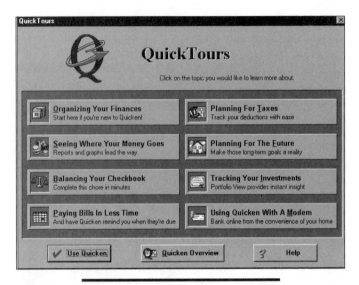

Figure 2.6 The QuickTours window.

The Main Quicken Window and HomeBase

Quicken is a modern Windows application, so you should be immediately comfortable with the display (Figure 2.7). At the top are a standard menu bar, and following current fashion, a toolbar of fast-action buttons, each sporting a colorful icon. Quicken calls this the *Iconbar*. The specific buttons you'll see on the iconbar depends on what version of Quicken 5 you have.

TIP

If the Iconbar isn't visible, click the circular **Iconbar** button near the top right of the Quicken window, shown here:

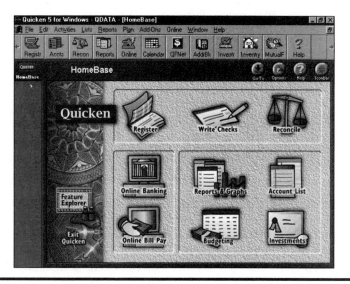

Figure 2.7 The Quicken window with HomeBase active in the main part
of the display. HomeBase looks slightly different if you have
the CD-ROM version of Quicken.

When you first use Quicken, a display called *HomeBase* occupies the
main part of the window (everything below the Iconbar except a nar-
row strip running down the left side of the screen). HomeBase is a
nice-looking central staging area that gives you quick access to all of
Quicken's major functions, including online financial transactions.

You're free to try out any of the buttons on HomeBase or the
Iconbar. However, since our primary job at this point is to get up and
running with online banking, we'll defer a discussion of these other
features until later. For now, a quick tip is in order:

TIP

As you use other parts of Quicken they usually take over the main
display area. But you can always return to HomeBase by clicking
the **HomeBase** button at the upper left, shown here:

Quicken
HomeBase

A summary of Quicken's extensive on-screen advice and help system appears in Chapter 3. For now, just remember that you can press the **F1** key any time to see a help message about the feature you're currently using.

Setting up for Online Banking

Once you have Quicken installed and have established an initial account, your next priority should be to set up for online banking. This involves these basic steps:

- Arrange with your bank or other institution to handle your online banking needs.
- If you want to manage your credit card records online, apply for a credit card with a participating institution.
- Set up your modem for use with Quicken.
- Set up an Intuit Membership, necessary for all online banking transactions via Quicken.
- Create the Quicken accounts you plan to use with online financial services, telling Quicken to activate the online capability for each account.
- If you plan to pay bills online, set up the payees to whom you'll be sending payments.

Making Arrangements with Your Bank

The first step in setting up for banking online is to request the service from your financial institution. To sign up, you'll need the institution's special phone number for such requests. Taking no chances with 800-number directory assistance, Intuit builds these phone numbers right into Quicken. Here's how you access them:

1. On the Quicken menu bar, click **Online** to open the Online menu.
2. Click **Financial Directory** to display a large window featuring the logos of many of the institutions providing online services via Quicken (Figure 2.8).

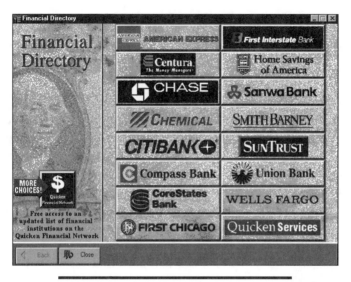

Figure 2.8 The Financial Directory lets you
access ads from a variety of institutions.

3. Click on any of the logos to see the institution's advertisement
   and get the necessary 800 number. Write down the number,
   then click **Back** to return to the main Financial Directory display.

4. If you want to comparison shop for online services, or have
   accounts at more than one institution, repeat step 3 as many
   times as you like. Then click **Close** to return to Quicken.

Now you can call the institution of your choice to sign up for online
services. If you have more than one account with an institution, be
sure to sign up each account. If you have accounts at more than one
institution you'll need to place more calls.

But in any case, you should receive a "welcome kit" for each
account within a few days. The kit includes literature detailing the
available services, any necessary forms to fill out, and an online services account information sheet. This lists the account number and a
special routing number you'll need to activate online activities.

Applying for an Online Credit Card

Several institutions offer credit cards with online features you can use via Quicken. In fact, there's even a Quicken Credit Card, sponsored by The Travelers' (for what it's worth, the Quicken card offers a fairly low interest rate).

With one of these credit cards, you can use your online access to obtain your monthly statement online, reconcile the statement against your own records, and send and receive messages with the sponsoring bank's customer service department.

Of course, you'll have to apply for the credit card first before you can use it with Quicken's online features. Contact the institutions listed in the Quicken Financial Directory to see which of them offers an online credit card.

Setting up Your Modem

Before Quicken can send and receive financial information over the telephone line, the program has to know how to communicate with your modem. Fortunately, setting up your modem for Quicken is easy—Quicken can usually complete the procedure automatically.

Before you start, be sure your modem is installed properly. If it is an *internal modem*—if it fits *inside* your computer's case—you may need to set switches on the modem or run special software to set the modem for the correct *COM port* (serial port address) of the computer. See the modem's manual for details. If you have an external modem with its own separate case, be sure the modem is connected properly to the computer, plugged in to the wall, and turned on.

NOTE

COM ports are "addresses" used by your computer to send and receive serial communications, the type used in modem transmissions. Each of your PC's physical serial ports—the ones on the back of the computer where you can in plug cables—is assigned to one of these COM port addresses. But additional COM ports are available for devices such as internal modems that plug into the slots inside your PC's case.

With these preliminaries out of the way, open the Online menu in Quicken and choose **Set Up Modem** at the bottom of the menu. Quicken immediately begins its automatic procedure for tracking down your modem and identifying its characteristics. A few moments later, it reports the results of its search in the box shown in Figure 2.9. If Quicken can't find your modem you'll see the same box with generic entries.

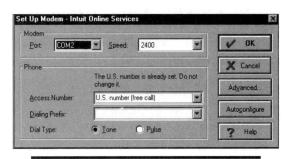

Figure 2.9 The Set Up Modem dialog box.

Check the settings Quicken displays against those of your modem. The Port setting must agree with that of your modem or online communications will be impossible. With some modems, Quicken may correctly identify the COM port but not the top modem speed, so change the speed entry if necessary.

As the box instructs you, don't change the entry in the Access Number area. At the bottom of the box, click the button corresponding to the type of phone line you have, tone or pulse (rotary).

If you want Quicken to dial a special number before the main telephone number, enter it in the Dialing Prefix area. For example, if you must dial 9 to access an outside line, type **9** in this area. Or, if your phone line has call waiting, enter the sequence you must dial to disable it so that incoming calls won't interrupt your online sessions. The prefix for disabling call waiting is often *70 for tone dialing lines or 1170 for rotary lines, but this depends on your locality, so check your phone book or call the phone company to be sure.

If you know your way around modem commands, you can enter special commands that Quicken should use for initializing and reset-

25

ting your modem. Click **Advanced** to access a box for this purpose. But if modem commands are Greek to you, don't worry—online banking should work fine with the generic commands Quicken enters automatically.

That's it. Click **OK** to close the Set Up Modem box.

Setting up Your Online Intuit Membership

As you learned in Chapter 1, all online financial information passes through a special service set up by Intuit, Quicken's publisher. To access this service you need to "join," receiving an Intuit Membership. When you do, you are assigned one membership number that applies to all of your online transactions, even if you have accounts with more than one financial institution. Setting up an Intuit Membership is free, at least as far as direct charges are concerned (refer back to Chapter 1 if you want to know where Intuit makes its money from your membership).

Since you'll need this master number for all online business, you should obtain it right away. Here's how:

1. Turn on your modem if necessary.

2. In Quicken, open the Online menu and choose **Intuit Membership—>Set Up**. Click **Set up new Intuit Membership** in the box that appears.

3. In the next box (Figure 2.10) fill in all your personal information, then click **OK**.

4. The next box (Figure 2.11) provides for security against the misuse of your online accounts. Before going further, choose a password for your Intuit membership. This can be any sequence of 4 to 16 letters, numbers, or other characters. Choose a password that isn't something that would be easy to guess, such as your daughter's name or your birthday, and is easy for you to remember. Contradictory criteria, I realize. At any rate, in the top two blank areas, type in the password twice—this ensures you've entered it correctly, since you can't see what you're typing here. Then type in your mother's maiden name in the space provided and click **Connect**—you're going online.

26

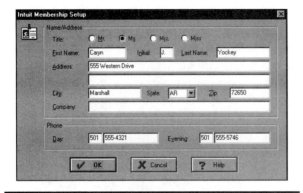

Figure 2.10 Set up your Intuit membership in this box.

Figure 2.11 Enter a password for your Intuit membership here.

In the interest of safeguarding your funds, it's probably best *not* to write down your password. If you can't trust your memory, store a paper copy of your password in a safe deposit box or perhaps at work or some other location.

5. Quicken dials the phone. In a few moments, you'll see a box reporting its progress in setting up your Intuit membership.

When the process is complete, Quicken hangs up the phone line and shows you your new Membership number, as shown in Figure 2.12 (as you can see, I changed the number to protect my own accounts). Although Quicken stores the number for you, you should write it down somewhere in case you need to access your membership from another computer.

Figure 2.12 Quicken reports your Intuit membership number in this box.

WARNING

Whatever you do, don't keep copies of your password and membership number in the same location.

6. Click **OK** to close the box and return to Quicken.

Setting up Your Quicken Accounts for Online Financial Services

Before you can use Quicken for any financial recordkeeping activities, you must create the Quicken accounts you need to adequately represent your financial universe. To use a Quicken account online, you must also tell Quicken to activate the account for that purpose.

If you're new to Quicken, by this point you should have just one Quicken checking account corresponding to the one at your bank. But

Quicken lets you have a whole range of different account types that match all your real-life financial dealings. You can create separate Quicken accounts to track your savings accounts and money market funds, your pocket cash, each credit card, and any major loans such as your home mortgage—up to 255 accounts in all.

Checking, Savings, Money Market, and Credit Card accounts can all be set up for online use in Quicken. You can set up as many accounts as you like for online banking, but each must correspond to a different real-life account, and you must make separate arrangements with the proper institution for each account (see the section "Making Arrangements with Your Bank" earlier in this chapter).

Activating Your Current Accounts for Online Use

To set up an existing account for online transactions you'll need the welcome kit you ordered from your financial institution. When the kit comes, find the online services account information sheet and keep it with you. Then proceed like this for each account:

1. Activate the Account List: From HomeBase, click **Account List**:

   or on the Iconbar, click the button labeled **Accts**:

   The Account List should look like the illustration in Figure 2.13.

2. In the list of accounts, locate the account you plan to set up for online transactions. Click once on the account so that it is highlighted.

3. Click the **Edit** button in the toolbar at the top left of the Account List. You'll see the Edit Bank Account window. As shown in Figure 2.14, this window opens to the summary panel, containing all the basic information about the account.

Figure 2.13 The Account List.

4. To activate online services for this account check one or both of the appropriate boxes in the middle of the summary panel: **Enable Online Banking** and **Enable Online Bill Payment**.

5. Click **Next** to move to a new panel of information pertinent to online services (Figure 2.15). It's time to get out that online services account information sheet you received from your financial institution. In the first blank area, use the drop-down list to pick the institution you hold the account with. Then type in the routing number and account number from the information sheet in the appropriate areas. If you're setting up something other than a checking account, select the proper type from the drop-down list in the Account Type area. Finally, type in your Social Security number and click **Done**.

6. Back at the Account List, you should see a little yellow lightning bolt in the row for the account, indicating the account is now activated for electronic, online transactions:

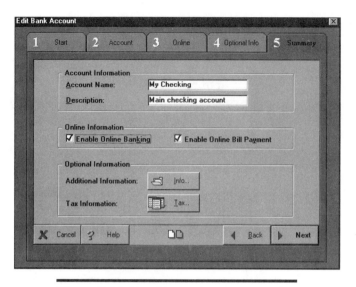

Figure 2.14 Use this panel to activate online services for an existing account.

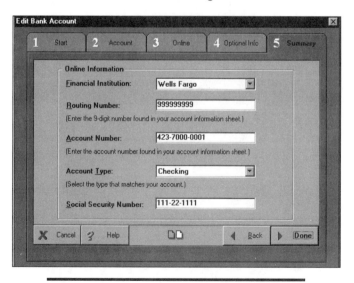

Figure 2.15 Enter the information needed for online banking in this panel.

Creating New Accounts

You can set up new Quicken accounts any time you need them. Quicken lets you create accounts that you plan to use online before you receive the welcome kit from your financial institution. That way, you can begin entering your previous and current records so that the account will be up to date when you activate it for online use. When the welcome kit comes, use the steps detailed in the previous section to activate the online functions.

Alternatively, you can wait to create the account until you receive the welcome kit. In this case, you activate it for online use during the process of creating the account.

Here are quick instructions for setting up additional accounts:

1. If it's not already visible, activate the Account List: From HomeBase, click **Account List**, or on the Iconbar, click the button labeled **Accts**.

2. Click the **New** button on the Account List toolbar. Quicken presents the Create New Account dialog box, shown in Figure 2.16. Click the button for the type of account you want to create (**Checking, Savings**, and so on).

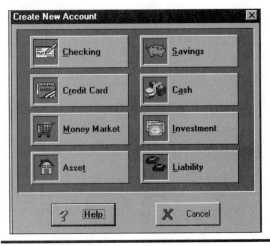

Figure 2.16 The Create New Account dialog box.

32

3. Quicken presents the first panel in the Account Setup window. This "EasyStep" window will walk you through the process painlessly. For new Quicken users, the steps are just like those you used to create your first account when you ran Quicken the first time—except that here, you can set up the account for online use as you create it.

4. Fill out the blank spaces in each panel as instructed, clicking **Done** to advance from one panel to the next.

5. When you get to the first Online panel for a Checking, Savings, or Money Market account (Figure 2.17), you can activate the account now if you've already received the welcome kit. Click the **Yes** buttons for either or both of the two types of online services you can use with the account: online banking and online bill payments. If you're creating a Credit Card account and have arranged with the issuing institution for online service, you just have one **Yes** button to click in the Online panel.

33

6. Once you've completed all the panels, click **Done** to create the account and return to the Account List.

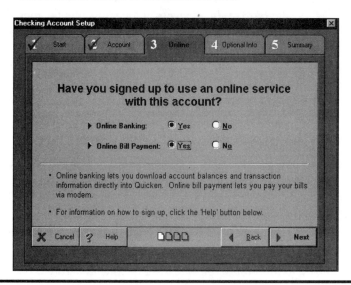

Figure 2.17 Use this panel in the Account Setup window to turn on online banking features for a new account.

Setting up to Pay Bills Online

Before you can pay a bill via an online "check," you must set up the recipient as an *online payee* so Quicken knows how to deliver the payment. Each of your payees (creditors) must be set up separately.

Remember from Chapter 1 that the funds for the bills you pay online are delivered in one of two ways. Many businesses are set up to receive electronic funds transfers from participating institutions. You'll receive a list of these "standard" payees via modem the first time you access your account online (I'll show you how to obtain the list of standard payees in a moment). For other payees, your bank will print and send a paper check.

At least one Quicken account must be activated for online bill payment before you can set up online payees (see the previous section for instructions on how to activate online bill payment). Once this is accomplished, grab all your recent bills and follow these steps:

1. To minimize the work you have to do, and to take advantage of electronic funds transfers, start by obtaining your institution's list of standard online payees. Open the Online menu and choose **Online Bill Payment**. Assuming you've followed all the preliminary steps above, you'll see the Online Bill Payment panel. With your modem ready to go, click the **Send** button at the lower right.

2. Quicken calls the service center and retrieves your institution's list of standard online payees, reporting its progress in a message box on the screen.

3. Open the Lists menu and choose **Online Payees**. You'll see the Online Payee List, shown in Figure 2.18. The picture shows the list with several payees already set up; the list will be empty the first time you open it.

4. With your stack of recent bills in hand, set up each creditor in turn by clicking the **New** button at the top of the Online Payee List window. You'll see a box like the one in Figure 2.19.

5. Enter the name of the payee in the top field, *Name*. If you completed step 1 above, you should click the arrow button to dis-

play the drop-down list of standard payees. If you find the name of the payee you're setting up, click it in the list. If not, click on the **Name** field and then type in the payee's full name as it should read on the check your institution will send.

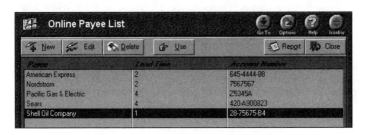

Figure 2.18 The Online Payee List.

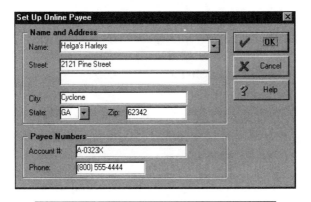

Figure 2.19 Set up online payees in this box.

6. Fill in the remaining information:

   • If you're setting up a standard payee, the only blank items you need to fill in are those in the Payee Numbers section. Type in the account number given you by that payee—not your own bank account number—and enter the payee's customer service telephone number.

- If you're setting up a payee from scratch, you'll need to enter the Payee Numbers mentioned above, as well as the payee's address.

7. Click **OK** when you're through to return to the Online Payee List. Repeat steps 4–6 for each online payee you want to set up.

NOTE

You can also set up online payees as you need them, while you're completing online "checks." When you enter a payee that hasn't been set up yet, Quicken presents you with the same box shown in Figure 2.19.

Summary

Once you've completed the steps outlined in this chapter, you're ready to begin transacting your financial business online. But before you do, spend some time getting up to speed with Quicken itself. You'll learn the basics in Chapters 3 and 4.

CHAPTER THREE:

Quicken Basics

This chapter offers a whirlwind tour of the most basic skills you need to keep track of your finances with Quicken: using the screen, accessing Help, and recording and "categorizing" transactions, including online payments.

One general note is in order before we begin. Quicken usually offers at least two (and often three or four) ways to complete a task or activate a given feature. Typically, you can:

- click a button (on the iconbar, on HomeBase, or on the toolbar at the top of the current window); or

- make a menu selection (from the menus at the top of the Quicken window, from the GoTo menu, or from one of the shortcut menu that pop up when you click the right mouse button); or

- press a keyboard shortcut (these are shown beside the choices on the main Quicken menus).

Since this book isn't intended as a complete Quicken reference, only the easiest methods are covered. Just be aware there are almost always multiple alternatives for accomplishing a particular goal.

Working with the Quicken Screen

You've already seen how Quicken's HomeBase screen gives you immediate, stylish access to the most commonly used Quicken functions. Again, to reach a Quicken function from HomeBase, you click the HomeBase icon for that function.

The Iconbar across the top of the Quicken window is another way to reach various functions when HomeBase isn't visible. Again, you just click a button to open the corresponding function.

NOTE

When you first install Quicken, the Iconbar doesn't include buttons for some of the most common functions such as writing checks. If you like, you can customize the Iconbar to give it just the buttons you want. Click **Options**, then **Iconbar**, and in the window that appears, choose which buttons to add and which to delete.

38

Another way to navigate to various Quicken functions is with the **Go To** button, present on most Quicken windows, including HomeBase:

When you click the **Go To** button, you get a menu listing many of the most common destinations in Quicken. Select an item on the menu and Quicken opens the appropriate window.

Using Quick Tabs

Once you've used a given Quicken function, it stays at the ready until you close it. You can return to that function by clicking on its **Quick Tab** at the left border of the screen. If only the HomeBase icon is showing, open another function or two using the techniques described above, then check the way the Quick Tabs area looks. Here's a sample:

NOTE

In earlier versions of Quicken, each Quicken function including HomeBase had its own separate window. If you prefer this arrangement, click **Options** —> **General**, and uncheck **Turn Quick Tabs Off**. But the new system makes for a much more orderly, less cluttered Quicken screen.

At the bottom of the Quick Tabs column along the left side of the Quicken window, you'll see a tab labeled To Do: `To Do!`

You click here to bring up the Quicken Reminders window, offering access to the various time-dependent items that Quicken keeps track of for you.

39

Getting Help in Quicken

You should never feel abandoned when you use Quicken: the program coddles you with a multitude of explanatory messages and tips, guides you through common procedures one simple step at a time, and provides you with the illustrated QuickTour of Quicken's main features (refer back to Figure 2.6). All this is in addition to a rich standard Windows Help system that provides detailed information on whatever function you're currently using.

With so much guidance available, you might even get confused about where to turn for help. Here's a quick guide to all the Quicken aids, including how to turn them off when possible should you find them too intrusive.

Quicken Tips Each time you start Quicken, you'll see a box displaying a brief tip on how to use a Quicken feature, as shown in Figure 3.1. Reading these tips is a good way to gradually familiarize yourself with Quicken's capabilities. Browse through additional tips by clicking **Next Tip** if you like, and click **Done** when you finish reading.

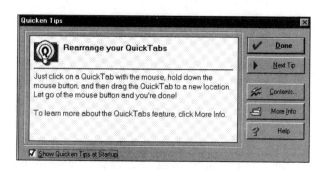

Figure 3.1 A Quicken Tip.

If you find the tips a nuisance, shut them off: uncheck the box at the bottom of the tip window labeled **Show Quicken Tips at Startup** (that is, click the box so that the check mark disappears). You'll still be able to see the tips by opening the Help menu and choosing **Quicken Tips**.

Flyover Help To see a brief explanation of the function of a button on a toolbar, just point the mouse at the button and hold it there for a few seconds. This works on the Iconbar at the top of the main screen, where the cryptic text of some of the buttons may leave you stumped. Here's an example of Flyover Help in action:

Flyover Help also works on the toolbars at the top of most Quicken windows, such as the account register, report windows, and so on.

Flyover Help isn't very obtrusive, but you can shut it off if it bothers you. Click the Options button, shown here:

to display the main Options dialog box. Then click **General** and in the next dialog box, uncheck the box labeled **Show Flyover Help in Toolbars**. Click **OK**, then **Close** to return to Quicken.

NOTE

Clicking the circular Options button shown earlier displays the main Options dialog box. Clicking the rectangular Options button, which you'll see on the toolbar in some windows such as the register, brings up a dialog box of options relating to that window.

Qcards Qcards are little windows containing instructions and tips on how to use the particular feature you're currently working with. Quicken displays the correct Qcard automatically, sprinkling them in various places throughout the program. However, they don't appear in every situation. Here's a sample Qcard:

> **Enter the name of the person or company you're writing the check to.**
>
> If this is a deposit, enter a description like 'Paycheck.'
>
> Quicken enters this payee in the drop-down list so you can use it more than once without typing it each time.
>
> Then press Tab to continue.   ? Help

41

Since Qcards cover up part of the screen, you'll want to turn them off as soon as you're comfortable with Quicken. To do so, open the Help menu and choose **Show Qcards** so that the check mark beside it is removed.

In the CD-ROM version of Quicken QCards are called Guide Cards, and have audio help as well as on-screen help.

QuickTour The QuickTour you ran into when you first ran Quicken is available any time. To run it, open the Help menu and choose **QuickTours**.

Help Quicken provides a standard Windows Help system. To see detailed information on the feature you're using at the moment, press **F1** or click the **Help** button at the top of the current window:

Help

or on the Iconbar. To browse the Help system as a whole, open the Help menu and choose the first item, **Quicken Help**. Help messages are displayed by the Windows Help viewer, and they work like the Help system in Windows itself.

Entering Financial Transactions in the Register

The register is the heart of Quicken—it's the place where Quicken records all of the transactions in your account. Figure 3.2 shows the register for the checking account created in Chapter 2.

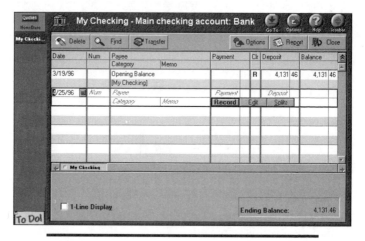

Figure 3.2 The Quicken checking account register.

The register looks very much like the paper register in your checkbook where you write down your checks and withdrawals. But it can store more information, and much more neatly.

Of course, Quicken provides a separate register for each of your accounts. The register looks a little different depending on which type of account (checking, credit card, investment, and so on) you're working with.

Just as in a paper register, the Quicken register gives you spaces to record the date, the check number (or the type of transaction for noncheck items), the payee, and the amount. The column labeled *Clr* is for marking cleared transactions when you balance your account. In addition, the Quicken register provides spaces in the second row for categorizing each transaction and typing in a memo.

The current account balance is displayed in the lower right. You can see more transactions at once by checking the *1-Line Display* box in the lower left.

If you have more than one Quicken account, you can switch to the register of another account by clicking the button labeled with the chosen account's name—these buttons are located in the row just below the list of transactions.

When you write checks or make online payments Quicken records them automatically in your register. But you'll need to enter most other types of transactions yourself.

Entering Deposits

The first skill to learn is how to enter transactions into the register. Although online banking can record many transactions for you, there are still times when you'll be entering transactions directly into the register. Besides, learning to enter transactions manually will give you a hands-on understanding of how the register works.

Let's say you plan to enter the following deposit into the register (you can use your own information if you prefer):

Date	Num	Payee	Deposit
10/18/96	DEP	Ketcham & Co.	$1644.00

To enter any new transaction, begin by finding the first empty transaction in the register. That should be easy, because it's always the last one in the register, and Quicken automatically highlights it with a bold outline whenever you first open the register.

In Quicken, you can work with only one transaction at a time. Quicken highlights the "active" transaction, drawing a heavy line around it and displaying it in a different color than the others. In addition, there's a set of three buttons, labeled *Record*, *Edit*, and *Splits* toward the right side of the active transaction.

If a different transaction is highlighted, move to the first empty transaction by scrolling with the scroll bar on the right, or just press **End** three times.

To record the new transaction, simply fill in the blanks (Quicken calls them *fields*) in the empty spaces. A small blinking vertical line, or cursor, indicates where you can enter information in a transaction:

1. When you begin a new transaction, the cursor should be in the **Date** field. If not, click the mouse over the **Date** field. Enter the date you made the deposit. You can type it in (type a / to move from month to day and day to year). Or you can click the little blue icon to the right of the **Date** field to pop up the date entry calendar, shown here:

   On the date entry calendar, move to the correct month using the arrows at the top left and top right. Then click on the date to enter it into the **Date** field.

TIP

You can adjust the date using shortcut keys. For example, to change it by one day press the + or – keys. See Quicken help for a complete list of these keys.

2. When you've finished with the date, press **Tab** to move to the **Num** field (you can click the mouse to move between fields instead, but pressing **Tab** is quicker and easier). If you were recording a check, you would enter the check number here. As soon as you get to the **Num** field, Quicken shows you a list of common transaction types. Select **Deposit** by clicking it with the mouse, and you'll see DEP appear in the field. If you prefer, you can type in **DEP** instead.

3. Press **Tab** to move to the *Payee* field. In deposit transactions, type the name of the company or person who wrote you the check or the source of the funds.

44

4. Press **Tab** to move past the *Payment* field to the *Deposit* field (with DEP in the *Num* field, Quicken knows to skip the *Payment* field). Now type in the dollar amount of your deposit. Alternatively, enter the amount with the pop-up calculator by clicking the small icon to the left of the Deposit field:

   To enter an amount, click the corresponding numerals, then click the large **Enter** button. The amount appears in the *Deposit* field.

NOTE

> You can use the calculator to add several numbers or perform other simple math functions—the total appears in the *Deposit* field when you're through.

45

5. Press **Tab** twice more to bypass the *Category* field and move to the **Memo** field. Here, you can type in a note to yourself about the transaction.

6. That's all it takes to enter a basic Quicken transaction (we'll look at how to use the all-important *Category* field shortly). Click the **Record** button—it's right there in the *Payment* field—or just press **Enter** to finalize your work and record the transaction.

   As soon as you record a transaction, Quicken adjusts the balance in your account accordingly, displaying the new total at the lower right of the register window.

Changing Information in a Transaction

If you find you've made a mistake in the field you're currently working on, fix it with the standard Windows text editing techniques: use the mouse or arrow keys to move the cursor to the incorrect characters, press **Del** or **Backspace** to remove them, and type in the right ones.

NOTE

You can nullify the most recent change you've made by choosing **Edit —> Undo** or pressing **Alt-Backspace**.

To correct an error in a different field in the current transaction, just click over the problem field. Quicken highlights the entire contents of the field—and with the highlight present, any new characters you type will erase and replace what was there. If you want to make fewer sweeping changes, don't type anything until the highlight is turned off. To do this, move to the problem characters by clicking again or using the arrow keys.

If the error is in a transaction you've recorded earlier, you must move to the transaction in question before you start changing things. Use the scroll bar or press the **Up** or **Down arrow** keys to move to the desired transaction so that the bold outline appears around its border. Once you've highlighted the transaction in this way, proceed with your changes as outlined above. To finalize your changes, click **Record** or simply move to another transaction (depending on how Quicken is set up, you may be asked to confirm your changes).

Entering Withdrawals, Cash Payments, and Handwritten Checks

To enter payment transactions such as checks you've written by hand, use the same procedure as for entering deposits—with these exceptions:

1. In the **Num** field, type in the check number, or for cash withdrawals, enter **ATM** or **CASH**.

TIP

If you're entering checks in sequence you can also select **Next Check #** or type in the first digit of the check number. Quicken is smart enough to fill in the next number in the sequence.

46

2. Enter the amount of your payment in the *Payment* field. Again, you can type in the amount or enter it using the pop-up calculator.

Again, record the transaction by pressing **Enter** or by clicking the button labeled **Record** just below the Payment amount.

Organizing Your Finances with Categories and Classes

If all you want Quicken to do is keep track of your total deposits and expenses, the basic transaction information discussed so far would be enough. But to tap Quicken's true power, you'll need to assign each transaction to a *category*, and perhaps to a *class* as well. Using Quicken categories and classes, you'll be able to see in detail where your money comes from, and where it goes.

47

Understanding Categories and Classes

Quicken's categories and classes have one basic function: they let you keep track of related transactions in groups. Categories and classes allow you to break down your expenses by type, so you can see how much you've spent on food, clothing, housing, and so on. For budgeting, categories and classes give you organized reports of your income and spending, so you'll know where to focus your efforts to earn more and spend less. At tax time, categories allow Quicken to break out your taxable income and deductible expenses just the way the IRS sees these amounts—all you have to do is transfer the totals to your tax forms.

TIP

One of the most important uses for Quicken categories is in preparing tax returns. But to take advantage of this capability you must set up Quicken categories for this purpose as described in Chapter 4.

Categories are your main Quicken tool for classifying your different income sources and expenses. Typical categories in the area of personal spending are housing, utilities, clothing, and auto expense. Income categories might include your salary, interest income, or income from a business, for example.

If you wish, you can subdivide the categories into smaller groups or *subcategories* for detailed accounting of a given type of financial activity. And you can organize categories into large collections called *supercategories* to help you track broad trends in your earning and spending.

Classes are a second and complementary way of classifying your transactions. They are best used to organize transactions according to a person, project, location, or time period.

Classes work hand-in-hand with categories to give you a more complete financial picture. For example, if you're using Quicken for your family checking account, you might set up different classes for you and your spouse. Then you'll know not only how much money is being spent in each category, but who is spending it! Another use for classes is to distinguish business and personal transactions in the same category.

Now that you've read in general terms about the use of categories and classes, we'll talk about the mechanics of working with them.

Assigning Categories and Subcategories to Transactions

Quicken supplies a whole set of generic categories that you can start using immediately. As you'll recall, when you set up your first account, you chose one of the two available sets of built-in categories: home categories or home and business categories (see the section on first time setup in Chapter 2).

To assign a category to a transaction you simply pick from the list of available categories. Let's say you've just fired up Quicken after depositing your paycheck and you want to record the following transaction:

48

Date	Num	Payee	Deposit	Category	Memo
10/24/96	DEP	ABC Industries	$1495.32	Salary	I need a raise!

You already know how to record the basic information. After you've entered the deposit amount, here's how to proceed with "categorizing" the transaction:

1. With the cursor in the *Deposit* field, press **Tab** to move to the *Category* field. As soon as you arrive there Quicken lists the available categories as shown here:

2. "Salary" should be visible near the bottom of the category list. If not, use the list's scroll bar to locate the Salary category in the list. Then click once on the category name to enter it in the *Category* field.

TIP

There's a faster way to enter categories if you're willing to use the keyboard. Just start typing the category name. Quicken's QuickFill feature finds the category that matches your typing and completes the rest of the entry for you. If Quicken's first guess isn't correct, just keep typing until the right category name appears in the field.

NOTE

When you record a transaction, Quicken warns you if you've forgotten to assign a category. You can override the warning, but your reports and graphs will be less accurate. Quicken labels totals for such transactions as "Other" in reports and as "Uncategorized" in graphs.

49

Assigning Subcategories

As you'll recall, subcategories let you organize categories into smaller divisions, all of which are related to the main category. A good example is the Auto category in Quicken's built-in category list. This category is intended for transactions that record expenses related to your car. But to allow you to break out the different types of car-related expenses—gasoline, insurance, and repairs, for example—Quicken includes subcategories such as Fuel, Insurance, and Service. If you use these subcategories routinely, you can produce reports and graphs showing you how much you spent on your car in total, with subtotals for each of the individual expense types.

Assigning a subcategory is exactly like assigning a regular category. If you want to try it, here's a sample transaction that records that last tank of gas you bought:

Date	Num	Payee	Amount	Category	Subcategory
2/18/96	Cash	Awful Oliver's Service Station	$18.79	Auto	Fuel

After entering the amount, move to the *Category* field. Scroll down through the list of categories to the Auto entry. Directly underneath it you'll see its subcategories, as shown here:

Just click on the **Fuel** subcategory to place it into the *Category* field. Here's how the transaction looks after you've recorded it in the register:

Notice how Quicken records the subcategory in the register. The main category, Auto, is listed first; then comes a colon, followed by the Fuel subcategory. If you want to, you can type in categories and subcategories yourself: first type the category name, then a colon, then the subcategory name.

In fact, with QuickFill, typing can be the fastest way to enter a long category/subcategory entry. Type the first letter or three of the main category until the correct entry appears in the *Category* field (the remaining letters that you didn't actually type will be highlighted). Now type a colon. Quicken automatically inserts the first subcategory for this category, which may be the one you want—in which case you're done. If not, start typing the subcategory name until the correct entry appears.

Customizing Your Categories

Although Quicken's built-in list of categories should cover most needs, the program gives you free rein to customize it. We'll take up that topic in Chapter 7.

Assigning Classes

Since classes are designed for customized classification schemes, Quicken doesn't come with any built-in class definitions—you have to create any classes you want from scratch. The techniques required to set up and assign classes are covered in Chapter 7.

Making Payments
Online—Or by Printed Check

Now that you understand the basics of entering transactions and assigning categories to them, you're ready to learn about making payments with Quicken. Paying your bills without the hassle of checks, envelopes, and stamps is one of the great conveniences of online banking. Quicken paper checks cost a lot more than online payments, too. But if you're not set up to pay bills online, you can use essentially the same techniques to write Quicken checks which you can then print out and mail.

Splitting Transactions

Since you're already familiar with the fundamentals of Quicken categories, this will also be your opportunity to learn more advanced categorization techniques. In real life, you'll often find that a single transaction covers items from a number of categories. To keep accurate records, you need Quicken's ability to *split* the transaction.

Of course, you can record nonsplit payment items, just as you did with the sample register deposit you made at the beginning of this chapter. To make a nonsplit payment, just choose the appropriate category for the entire transaction in the *Category* field.

52

Let's say you visit the JumboGiant "superstore" one weekend and come away with food for your family, computer supplies for your business, and a new faucet for the kitchen sink, paying for the purchase with your JumboGiant credit card. When the $243.66 bill comes in, you decide to avoid interest charges by issuing an online payment to cover the whole purchase. Splitting the transaction lets you do this while you continue to track your spending on a category-by-category basis.

Although the example transaction shown here is a payment, the split transaction feature works identically with deposits. When a single deposit contains more than one income source, record it as a split deposit transaction. In the register, the **Splits** button resides just below the *Deposit* field in the transaction you're currently working with.

Writing a Check, Online or Otherwise

Before you can make any payments online, you must arrange with your bank to use online bill paying, set up Quicken for this function, and set up the payees (recipients) for your online "checks." Setting up for online bill payment is covered fully in Chapter 2.

Setting up a Sample Online Payee

If you want to practice online payments with the following example, set up a dummy online payee (this step isn't necessary for printed checks). You can use the following sample information:

JumboGiant Superstore
444 West Alum Road
Hanover, CT 13241

Acct number: X222000
Customer service phone number: 202-555-7799

To enter the information, open the Lists menu, choose **Online Payees**, and then click the **New** button. Use the information above to fill out the box that appears (Figure 2.19), then click **OK** to record the new payee. Finally, click **Close** to remove the Online Payee List from the screen.

53

Writing the Check

Now you should be ready to write an online payment (or a check) to pay that credit card bill. Your first order of business is to switch to the check writing window, shown in Figure 3.3.

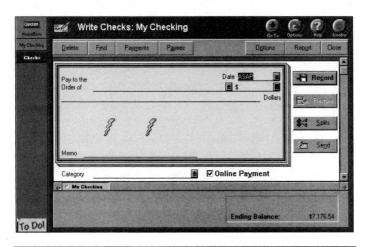

Figure 3.3 Use this window to write online payments or printed Quicken checks.

To move to the Write Checks window, click the **Go To** button: and choose **Write Checks** from the menu that appears. Alternatively, if you're already at HomeBase, it's easier to click the **Write Checks** icon there:

Once the Write Checks window is visible, be sure a new blank check is on the screen; if not press **End** to display one.

NOTE

> If you were recording a check you wrote at the store, you would enter it from the register, but the procedure for splitting the transaction would be the same.

The picture in Figure 3.3 shows the way an on-screen check looks if you're paying bills online. Those two lightning bolts in the middle of the screen are the giveaway—they're missing from checks to be printed, replaced by an *Address* field.

Notice also the checkbox labeled *Online Payment* appears beneath the screen check (this box appears only if at least one account has been activated for online bill payment). You can switch back and forth between online payments and printed checks by checking or clearing this box.

1. Quicken sets the *Date* field to **ASAP** if you're filling out an online payment or today's date for printed checks. You can change the entry here as you like. The entry **ASAP** means that after receiving the payment request, your bank will pass along the online payment to the payee as soon as possible. If you enter a later date, the bank will wait to transfer the funds electronically until that date or will issue a paper check so that it arrives on approximately that date. (See Chapter 5 for details on dating online payments.)

2. Make the check payable to **JumboGiant**. If you're making an online payment, the QuickFill feature will scan your online

payee list as you type, completing the payee name as soon as you type the first letter or two. Press **Tab** to move to the *Amount* field.

NOTE

If you're making an online payment to a payee you haven't yet set up in the Online Payee List, just type in the name on the Payee line of the screen check. When you **Tab** past the *Payee* field, Quicken will ask if you want to set up a new online payee. Click **Set Up** to display the Set Up Online Payee window (Figure 2.19).

3. Now type in the total amount of the payment, **$243.66** in the example. Notice that as soon as you advance to the next field (by pressing **Enter** or **Tab**), Quicken converts the numeric amount into words, just as you would do when writing a paper check.

4. If you're making an online payment the next field is *Memo*—skip to step 5. If you're writing a check to be printed, there's a large field labeled *Address* in the middle of the screen check. You would use this area to type in the address of the payee if you plan to mail it in one of those windowed envelopes, or if you want to store the address for reference. Otherwise you can leave it blank.

5. If you like, use the *Memo* field to type in a note applying to the payment as a whole, something like **Saturday shopping spree**.

Splitting the Payment Transaction

That completes the preliminaries. Now you're ready to split the payment. Click the **Splits** button—again, it's just below the *Deposit* field for the correct transaction. You'll see the Splits window, shown in Figure 3.4.

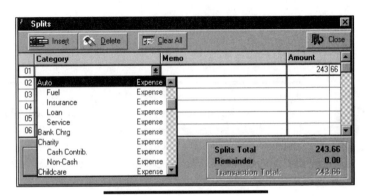

Figure 3.4 The Splits window.

56

NOTE

You can also open the splits window by moving to the *Category* field and choosing the **Split Transaction** item at the top of the QuickFill category list.

In essence, the Splits window is a simple table with rows for the individual items in the transaction (in this example, the groceries, the faucet, or the supplies). In each row, you enter a separate category, an individual memo if you like, and the item's dollar amount. Note that Quicken has transferred the total amount of the check to the Amount column in the first row. Like other Quicken windows, the Splits window also has buttons along the top and bottom.

If you want to continue with the example, here's a category-by-category breakdown of the sample purchase:

Category	Memo	Amount
Groceries	Weekly groceries	$112.67
Home repairs	Faucet for kitchen sink	$84.95
Supplies	Computer disks and printer paper	$32.25
Sales tax		$13.79

Let's walk through the steps needed to split the transaction:

1. The cursor should be blinking in the first row in the Category column. You make category (and class) entries here the same as you do when filling the *Category* field in the register transaction: by picking a category from the list that automatically appears or by typing the first letter or two and letting QuickFill rush in to complete the entry.

2. Now make an entry for the first part of the split, the one covering your food purchase at JumboGiant. Enter the category **Groceries** in the first column. Next, move to the Memo column and make an entry if you like. Finally, in the Amount column, type in the amount for this item (**$112.67**), replacing the original entry.

3. Press **Tab** again when you finish the Amount column. The cursor then moves to the Category column for the second row of the split. In the sample payment, that would be the faucet. Before going further, look in the *Amount* column for this item—you'll see it contains what's left of the original check total after the groceries purchase has been subtracted. Now enter the item details. The *Category* field should read **Home Repairs**. Press **Tab** to move to the Memo column; an appropriate memo here would be—you guessed it—**Sink**. **Tab** over to the Amount and type in the cost for the sink, **$84.95**, and press **Tab** to move to the third line.

4. Complete the entries for the third and fourth parts of the split using the information above. You shouldn't have to change Quicken's automatic entry in the Amount column for the last line—at this point, with the amounts for each item accounted for, what's left is the sales tax you paid. When you press **Tab** to finish your last item, your screen should look like Figure 3.5.

5. When all four lines in the window are complete, click **OK** to finish the entry. Quicken asks if you want to keep the changes. You'll return to the Write Checks window. Here, the *Category* field will show **-SPLITS-**. Press **Enter** to record the transaction and display a new empty check.

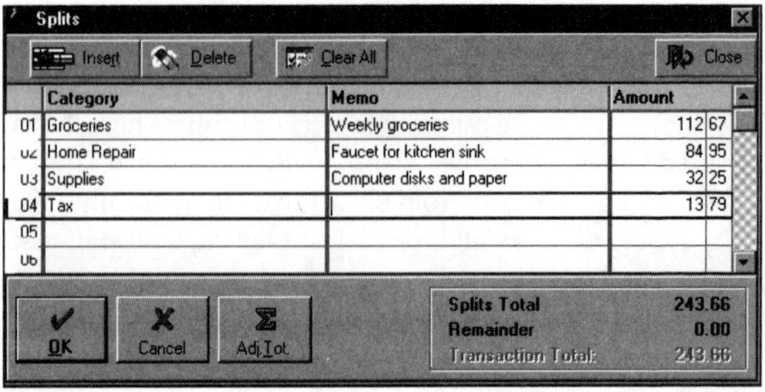

Figure 3.5 The completed Splits window showing the sample transaction detail.

Payment Transactions and the Register

As soon as you record a payment transaction on the Write Checks window, Quicken places the transaction in your register. To prove it, move to the register entry for the check you just wrote. Click the *Quick Tab* for the register in question or click the **Go To** button and choose **Register**. You may need to scroll in the register to find the correct transaction.

Notice the **-SPLITS-** entry in the Category column. If you click the small **Splits** button below the transaction amount Quicken will display the same Splits window you used to enter the splits in the first place. (Again, you can use the **Splits** button to record splits for any register transaction, including income items.)

Back at the register window, notice too that Quicken has filled in the Num column for you (it reads *Send* for online payments, *Print* for checks). Here's what's going on: Quicken uses these designations to keep track of payment transactions you've written but not yet sent. When you're ready to send payments, Quicken scans your entire register for any payments not previously sent. Once a payments is sent,

Quicken changes the register entry in the Num column to **EFT** (electronic funds transfer) for online payments or the actual check number for printed checks.

Sending the Payment

Once you've written out an online payment or check, you're eventually going to have to part with those funds. Of course, the steps required here will vary depending on whether you've written an online payment or a check to be printed.

One thing that is essentially the same for both types of payments is that Quicken expects you to handle batches of payments in one operation. Quicken will assume you want to send all the pending online payments or print all the unprinted checks. However, you'll be given a chance to select just those items you actually want to send.

Sending Online Payments

To send online payments in the Write Checks window, be sure that the **Online Payment** box below the screen check is checked. Click **Send**. Quicken has your modem dial the Intuit service center and make the payments. See Chapter 5 for details.

Printing a Paper Check

Printing paper checks requires some preliminary work. Obviously, you have to buy the checks first. For personal use with a laser or inkjet printer, I recommend getting the wallet checks that come three to a page—they're the least expensive. Checks for dot matrix printers are also fairly reasonable.

Next you must set up to print the checks. Quicken can print checks on any printer that works with Windows. Your setup tool is the Check Printer Setup window, shown in Figure 3.6.

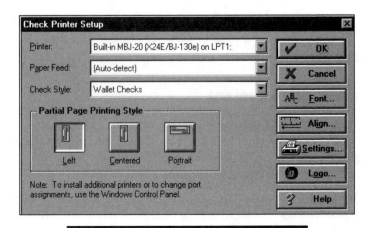

Figure 3.6 The Check Printer Setup window.

Since this book concentrates on online banking, we won't go into the Check Printer Setup window in depth. Here are the essentials: to access this window, open the File menu, choose **Printer Setup**, and in the secondary menu that appears, choose **Check Printer Setup**. In the window, select the printer you want to use to print checks, the type of checks you're using, and the font you want printed on them.

Before you actually print any checks, be sure printing alignment is correct by printing some sample checks (I strongly recommend you consult Quicken's Help on check alignment for vital tips on this process). And if you want a printed logo added to your checks, use the **Logo** button to select a graphic file.

Once you've set up your printer, print the paper checks as follows:

1. In the Write Checks window, be sure you're working with paper checks—if the box labeled **Online Payment** beneath the screen check has a check mark, click the box to clear it. Now click **Print**. Quicken presents the Select Checks to Print window (Figure 3.7).

2. At the top of the window Quicken provides a space to type in the number of the first check in the sequence—look for this on the blank checks you'll be printing. Quicken numbers subse-

quent checks in order, then remembers the next number for the next time you print checks. But you can always change the check number if a sheet of checks gets lost or damaged.

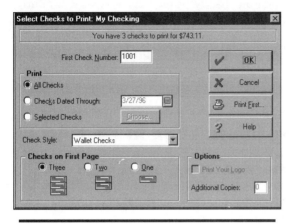

Figure 3.7 This window initiates check printing.

3. Next are a set of buttons that let you tell Quicken which checks to print: all of them, those dated through a date you specify, or particular checks you specify from a list.

4. In the Check Style area, you can override the type of checks you selected in the Check Printer Setup window (*Standard*, *Voucher*, or *Wallet*).

5. At the bottom of the window, the buttons labeled **Checks on First Page** are handy when you have a partially used sheet of checks left over from your last session. If so, click the button for the number of checks on the sheet, one or two.

6. The **Print Logo** box is only active if you defined a printable logo when setting up to print checks, as discussed above. Check the box to print the logo on your checks.

7. When you've finished making choices, ready your printer and click **OK**. Quicken starts printing the checks immediately, unless you've told it to print selected checks. In that case, you get a list of unprinted checks from which you can select.

61

8. Quicken displays a little box labeled *Did check(s) print OK?* Examine the printed checks. If everything looks right, click **OK** to tell Quicken that all went well. If not, type in the number of the first incorrectly printed check. Quicken returns you to the Select Checks to Print window, where you can try again.

Now it's up to you to stuff the checks into envelopes and send them on their way.

Finding Information in Your Accounts

Once you've entered a month or two's worth of financial records, finding a specific transaction gets a lot more difficult. Quicken's Find feature will search through your register to locate transactions by any of the information they contain.

For example, let's say you want to locate the payment to the JumboGiant store. Begin by opening the Edit menu and clicking on **Find** (not Find/Replace). Alternatively, you can simply press **Ctrl-F**. You'll see the box shown in Figure 3.9.

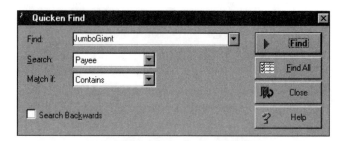

Figure 3.9 The Find dialog box.

Enter the information you're searching for—"JumboGiant" in this example—in the Find field. The next field, *Search*, offers a drop-down list of the fields Quicken should check when looking for a match. Initially, this field is set to All Fields, meaning that the search would pick up transactions that show "JumboGiant" in the Payee, Category, or Memo fields. If you like, you can further refine the search by selecting the Payee option from the drop-down list. Leave the *Match* If field set to *Contains* if you want Quicken to find all transactions containing the search entry anywhere within the chosen field(s). The other options in the drop-down list here should be self-explanatory.

You're ready to start the search. When you click **Find**, Quicken locates and highlights the next register transaction matching your request. Normally, Quicken searches "forward" in the register (toward the end of the list). To search backward, click the **Search Backwards** box. To see a list of all matching transactions at once, click the **Find All** button instead. The list appears in a separate large window.

You can use the Find/Replace feature to change information in transactions matching your criteria. Choose **Find/Replace** from the Edit menu. The top part of the box offers the same three fields as the Find box, and they work the same way. After you've filled them out, click **Find All**. When the list of matching transactions appears in the lower part of the window, complete the remaining two fields: In Replace, indicate which field you want to change in the found transactions; in With, enter the new information you want the chosen field to contain.

Backing Up Your Records

Keeping extra copies of your financial records is always a good practice, and it's doubly important when you use a computer. Although your PC is very reliable, the disks on which you store your data are perhaps its most vulnerable components. Even if they don't break down prematurely they eventually wear out. Besides, there's always the possibility of human error (accidentally deleting the files from your disk) and of loss or damage to your computer from another source (theft, fire, or your two year-old-child pouring water onto the machine).

You must resolve to make copies regularly of all your Quicken accounts onto backup disks. Plan to do this once a month at a bare minimum. Depending on how often you use Quicken, and how detailed and crucial your records are, you may need to back them up weekly or even daily. As long as you make backups faithfully, if something ever does go wrong with your PC you'll be able to retrieve most or all of your records from the backup copies. Without the copies, your records will be gone forever.

Fortunately, Quicken makes it extremely easy to save backup copies of your accounts onto a diskette, and the process takes only a few seconds. You can also back up your records on any other location that is accessible as a disk drive in Windows, such as a tape drive, a removable cartridge drive, or an optical drive. (You can also choose a different hard disk as the backup destination, but I recommend against this—your files won't be protected against theft or major damage to the whole computer.)

Find a blank, formatted diskette (or other backup medium) and after labeling it as your Quicken backup, place it in the drive. Now open the File menu and click **Backup**. You'll see the Select Backup Drive box (Figure 3.10)

64

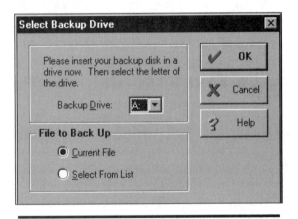

Figure 3.10 The Select Backup Drive dialog box.

In the Backup Drive field, use the drop-down list to choose the letter name of the drive where your backup diskette or other medium is located. The radio buttons in the *File to Back Up* field let you specify whether to back up the file that's currently in use or to choose a file for back up from a list of those available. Click **OK** after making your selections. (If the chosen drive letter belongs to anything other than a floppy drive, you'll next be asked to type in the directory, or folder, where you want to store the backup files. Do so and click **OK** again.)

As it works, Quicken informs you that it's backing up the selected file. When the process is complete you're notified, then returned to Quicken. If your records are ever lost or damaged, you can retrieve the backup copies with the **Restore** command, also on the File menu.

Summary

In this chapter you got your feet wet with Quicken—or you had a refresher course that also brought you up to speed with what's new in Quicken 5 (for 96). You should now be comfortable with maneuvering in the Quicken screen, using Help when you're stuck, and entering register transactions and payments. In learning to use categories and classes, you can now bring to bear some of the most important Quicken techniques for managing your finances—the effort you've made will pay off as you produce informative reports and graphs.

65

CHAPTER FOUR:

Online Banking with Quicken

Until the advent of online banking you would receive a single monthly statement from your bank. Although these printed statements contain plenty of information, they leave a lot to be desired—mainly because they only come once a month, and they're always a week or more out of date by the time you get them in the mail.

Of course, it has always been possible to run down to the bank to get more current information on your account. More recently, telephone service centers have become the rule, allowing you to call in for your current balance or to see whether a given check has cleared. But none of these services can match Quicken's online banking for convenience and information quality.

With online banking, you're not stuck trying to jot down stray figures on scratch paper while the bank agent rattles them off. Instead, whenever you like, and without waiting for the "next available representative," you get a complete, up-to-date, legible, written report on your account and all its transactions via your modem.

In more detail, here are some of the things you can accomplish with online banking:

- obtain your current account balance
- check to see which checks have cleared the bank
- automatically update your Quicken accounts with records of transactions other than Quicken payments (even without online banking, Quicken records online bill payments and Quicken checks for you)
- transfer money between accounts at the same financial institution
- speed the process of balancing, or *reconciling*, your checkbook
- exchange messages with your financial institution about your account

The bad news? You should still balance your checkbook every month, just to be sure that you and the bank agree. But with Quicken, the process is almost painless.

Setting up for Online Banking

Before you can start using online banking you must make a few preparations. The steps were detailed in Chapter 2, but here they are again in brief:

1. *Set up your modem.* If you haven't yet set up your modem, open the Online menu and choose **Set Up Modem** to do so.

2. *Obtain an Intuit membership.* You need an Intuit membership no matter which financial institution you bank with. If you haven't set one up, be sure your modem is on, open the Online menu, and choose **Intuit Membership —> Set Up**.

3. *Arrange with your bank to activate online banking.* If you have more than one bank account, you must separately activate each account you'll be using with online banking. You'll receive instructions and a special routing number from the bank.

4. *In Quicken, turn on online banking for the corresponding Quicken account.* In the Account List window, find the Quicken checking

account representing the bank account you've activated for online banking. Edit the account setup so that the box labeled **Enable Online Banking** is checked. (If you don't already have a Quicken account for the bank account in question, create one, making sure you've enabled online banking). Quicken will then ask you to enter information about your online bank account, including the institution, account number, and the routing number supplied by the bank.

Obtaining Your Current Statement

Once you're up to speed with online banking, using Quicken to get your current account statement will become a routine activity. Whether you obtain your statement daily, every Friday, or simply whenever you need it, you'll find that having up-to-date information sharpens your financial awareness and makes you a better money manager.

69

NOTE

The information you'll receive in an online statement is up-to-date, but it's not up-to-the-minute. In general, the statement represents the status of your account as of the closing the day before you make your request. During normal work weeks, most institutions post data Tuesday through Saturday—so if you get an online statement on Sunday, you have to wait until Wednesday to get new information.

Here's how to obtain an account statement covering all the accounts you have at a particular institution:

1. To display the Online Banking window (Figure 4.1), open the Online menu and choose **Online Banking** (if you're already at HomeBase, you can click the **Online Banking** icon):

Online

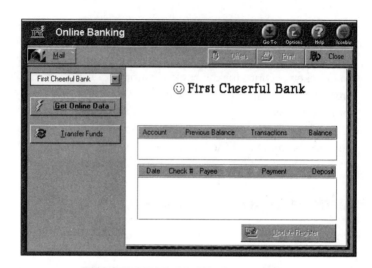

Figure 4.1 The Online Banking window.

2. In the Financial Institution field, choose the bank or other institution where you have the account from the drop-down list.

3. Click the button labeled **Get Online Data**. You'll be asked to type in your PIN (personal identification number) for this account. If the bank has supplied a new PIN for the account, you'll be asked to enter a new PIN of your own choosing. Be sure you memorize your PIN, but protect any written copy of the number very carefully.

4. Click **OK** to proceed. Quicken activates your modem, connecting to the online banking center.

5. When the call is complete, Quicken displays a Transmission Summary window, confirming that your request for account information was carried out. After a quick look at the summary, click **OK**.

You should be back at the Online Banking window. As shown in Figure 4.2, the top part of the window lists all the accounts you have with the institution. For each account, you see the balance the last time you obtained an online statement (this is 0 the first time you connect), the number of transactions that have occurred since then, and the current balance.

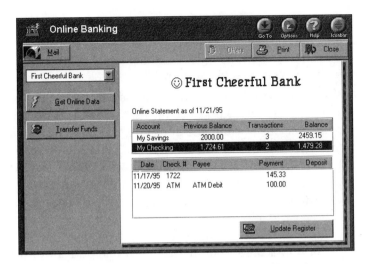

Figure 4.2 The Online Banking window after receiving account information.

To see the transactions from a particular account, highlight that account in the upper part of the Online Banking window. Quicken displays the transaction details below, showing you all transactions that have occurred in the account since your last time online. Just as on a paper statement, transactions are listed in the order they cleared the bank with the most recently cleared transactions at the bottom of the list.

Updating Your Quicken Register with Online Records

Quicken can add transactions received in your online statement to your register. This is great for Quicken users—it means you no longer have to type in transactions from paper records.

Let's postpone further discussion for a bit and begin with the technique:

1. *Retrieve your current account statement* following the steps in "Obtaining your Current Statement," earlier in this chapter.

When the Online Banking window displays the updated account information, you're ready (if the window lists more than one account, highlight the account you want to work with in the top portion of the window).

2. *Click the* **Update Register** *button* at the lower right of the Online Banking window. Quicken compares the transactions in your online statement with those in your register, and then displays the new window shown in Figure 4.3. The top part of the Update Register window lists "new" transactions. These are the transactions from your online statement for which no matches were found among those already in your Quicken register. Quicken will add them to the register for you if you give the word. At the bottom of the window, Quicken displays the number of transactions from the statement that do match existing register entries.

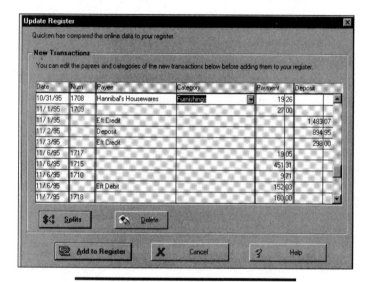

Figure 4.3 The Update Register window.

3. *Edit the new transactions as necessary before adding them to your register.* The statement doesn't provide payee information for

handwritten checks, so you'll have to add this. You'll also need to categorize all the new transactions. If you're sure a transaction listed here is already entered in your account, delete it from the list of new transactions by highlighting the transaction and clicking the **Delete** button.

4. *Click the **Add to Register** button* when all the new transaction information is correct. Quicken enters the transaction in your register and returns you to the Online Banking window.

5. If you have additional accounts to review, take care of each in turn by highlighting it in the account list and repeating steps 2–4. When you're through reviewing the online statement, click **Close** to remove the Online Banking window.

As Quicken adds the new transactions to your register it marks them as "cleared," placing a "c" in the register's Clr column. Quicken also marks as cleared any existing register transactions that matched transactions in the online statement (see Figure 4.4). Marking a transaction as *cleared* means that it has already been posted to your account. In the case of checks, this alerts you to an important fact: the funds in question have actually left your account. We'll return to this point in a moment (see "Checking for Cleared Checks," later in this chapter).

73

Date	Num	Payee		Payment		Clr	Deposit	Balance	
		Category	Memo						
11/13/95	1721	Chevron		16	99	c		669	47
		Auto:Fuel							
11/14/95	1714	Mervyn's		136	82	c		532	65
		Clothing							
11/14/95	1723	Half Moon Bay Nursery		8	19	c		524	46
		Gardening							
11/15/95	1725	El Granada Hardware		18	55	c		505	91
		Gardening							
11/16/95	ATM	Lucky		57	07	c		448	84
		Groceries	Star Pos 150						
11/16/95	1724	New York Fabrics		48	28	c		400	56
		Gifts							

Figure 4.4 The checking account register showing several transactions cleared after updating the register from an online banking statement.

NOTE

To view the changes Quicken has made in your records, switch to the register: Click the **Register** button on the Iconbar or in HomeBase. Then, if the correct account isn't already displayed, click the button for the one you want in the account selector just below the main section of the register.

Why Update Your Register with Online Records?

Without online banking, Quicken offers a great system for tracking your finances, but it requires extra work to maintain complete records. The reason? Even if you use Quicken checks to pay your bills, you have to type in copies of all other transactions yourself. For example, when you write a check by hand at the grocery store or dry cleaners, you must duplicate the information from your paper check register in the register in Quicken. If you buy something in cash, or make a deposit, you have to copy the paper receipt to a Quicken transaction.

Much of that duplication of effort vanishes when you use online banking. When you write a check by hand, you should still write it down in your paper checkbook. But now you can let Quicken insert the corresponding register transaction from your online statement. Of course, you'll want to check the bank's transaction information against your paper record, and you still must assign a payee and category to the transaction once it arrives in Quicken using the Update Register window (Figure 4.3).

Checking for Cleared Checks with Online Banking

Sometimes it's vital to know whether a particular check has cleared the bank. When a creditor insists that he never got your last payment and you're *sure* you paid the bill, a good way to begin your investigation is by checking with your bank to see if the check has been cashed.

With online banking, you can have your answer fast, without fighting traffic, or fighting your way through the bank's automated telephone answering system ("please do press 5 for more options").

NOTE

The method for finding out whether a check has cleared works for payments you write with Quicken's online bill payment service (see Chapter 5), as well as for printed checks and those you write by hand.

To see whether a check has cleared the bank, the place to start is your Quicken register. If you can't spot the check in question immediately, locate it by clicking the **Find** button and searching for the payee.

Examine the entry in the Clr field. An entry of **c** or **R** means that the check has been cashed and has cleared the bank (you'll learn the difference between the "c" and "R" entries in the section on reconciling below).

If the Clr field is empty, however, you can't be sure about the check's status until you go online. The same is true if the check doesn't appear in the register at all (which means you're investigating a check you wrote by hand but never entered in Quicken). In either case, use the technique laid out above to connect with the online banking center and retrieve your current statement.

When you return to the Online Banking window, highlight the account on which the check is drawn. Now examine the list of new transactions shown in the lower part of the window. If the check shows up in the list, you have your answer—it has cleared.

If the check isn't listed, however, you know that as of the statement's closing, the check hadn't cleared the bank. Since today's online statement reflects activity in your account through yesterday, it's still possible the check has cleared very recently.

Once you've come this far, go ahead and update your register, adding any new transactions to your register and marking all transactions from the new statement as cleared. See the section on updating your register earlier in this chapter.

Transferring Funds between Accounts

Online banking lets you move funds between two accounts you hold at the same financial institution. Theoretically, you should be able to transfer funds between any two accounts, although some financial institutions may limit the types of accounts you can use with online banking.

Why Keep Separate Accounts?

There are a variety of good reasons to split up your funds over separate accounts. Here are a few:

- *To make more money.* Checking accounts often pay no interest, and even when they do, the rate is lower than what you earn in a savings or money market account. It's smart to keep only enough funds in your checking account to pay your bills, parking the rest in an account paying a higher rate.

- *To maximize the amount protected by federal deposit insurance.* Because of the laws regulating financial institutions, you may be able to insure much more money if you divide up your funds over several accounts. Check with the bank or your tax accountant.

- *To help you keep track of funds intended for different purposes.* Although it's fairly simple to manage money earmarked for distinct objectives in the same account, you may find it easier to set up one account for each major segment or purpose. This approach can help enforce discipline, making it a little harder to spend money impulsively.

However, once you've established a number of accounts with your bank, it becomes important to manage them actively. Whenever your checking account balance nears "empty"—or perhaps when it drops close to the cutoff for fee-free checking—you'll want to infuse funds from other accounts. Conversely, after a big deposit into your checking account, you should move any excess to an account paying a higher rate. And every month you'll be making your regular contributions to any special accounts for say, retirement or college savings.

You'll learn in Chapter 8 all about how to keep records in Quicken of money transfers between bank accounts, and between bank accounts and other financial resources such as cash. Here, we'll concentrate on the procedures you'll use to instruct your financial institution to transfer the money itself.

Transferring the Funds

Once you've decided which account you're moving the funds from and which one they're headed for, follow these steps:

1. Open the Online menu and choose **Bank Online**.

2. In the Bank Online window, select the financial institution with which you hold the accounts in the drop-down list.

3. Click **Transfer Funds**. Quicken displays the Transfer Funds Between Accounts box, shown in Figure 4.5.

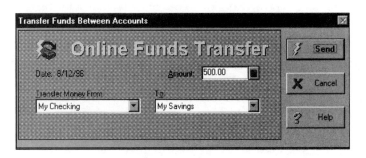

Figure 4.5 The Transfer Funds Between Accounts box.

4. The box lists all your accounts with this institution twice, in separate lists labeled *Transfer Money From* and *Transfer Money To*. Highlight the account you've chosen in each list.

5. Type in the amount you want to transfer or enter it with the pop-up calculator.

6. With your modem ready, click the **Transmit** button. Quicken goes online and sends in your instructions, adding register transactions to your corresponding Quicken accounts. Assuming the "from" account contains adequate funds, the transfer will be complete within a day. If not, you'll be notified that the transfer didn't go through.

Reconciling (Balancing) Your Checking Account

If you're a responsible money manager, you're used to spending a few minutes each month comparing your monthly bank statement to your own checkbook records to see which checks have cleared, and to catch any overcharges or unexpected fees. Most important, you want to see that the bottom lines match—that you and your bank agree about how much money was in your account at the time the statement was issued. This is called *balancing* a checkbook. The more accurate term is *reconciling* since you are checking your records against the bank's, and trying to resolve or reconcile any discrepancies. With Quicken, this little bit of required drudgery becomes almost effortless.

To some degree, the availability of a new online bank statement nearly every day changes the function of checkbook balancing. Although I'm sure any accountant would insist that you still formally reconcile your accounts on a regular basis, it's hardly as critical if you're keeping close tabs via daily or weekly online updates. Reconciling becomes a backup safeguard rather than the primary means to catch errors in your records.

Balancing Against Paper or Online Bank Statements

At any rate, you can pick between two approaches to reconcile an online banking account. *You can only choose one of these methods*—you'll get inaccurate results if you try to mix the two. Here are the options:

- *Reconcile against your paper statement.* Probably the safest method is to continue reconciling against your monthly paper statement. You can still obtain online statements as often as you like during the month, and you can still use them to update your account, allowing Quicken to mark transactions on each statement as cleared in your register. When your paper statement arrives, you get an extra chance to check your records against those of your bank via "formal" balancing. I recommend this approach.

- *Reconcile against your online statement.* The alternative is to reconcile to your online statements exclusively. With this approach, you'll be reconciling against one of the same online statements you retrieve for less formal account updates. The only difference is that when you reconcile, Quicken lets you again review the transactions marked as cleared since the last time you reconciled, including those cleared when you retrieved previous online statements. In this case, since you're reconciling against the same information you use to update your accounts, you give up the extra level of protection afforded by the paper statement. But this is definitely the easier approach.

An Overview of the Balancing Process

Here, in a nutshell, is how balancing or reconciling your accounts works with Quicken. There are four basic steps:

1. Starting from the register of the account you want to reconcile, initiate the reconciliation process.

2. Enter essential information from your bank statement, such as the beginning and ending balances for the period your statement covers and any service charges, fees, or interest payments. If you're reconciling against your online statement, Quicken completes this step for you.

79

3. Using this information, Quicken displays a list of the transactions that have not been previously reconciled. Your job is to mark as cleared the transactions that appear on your bank statement. If you have been updating your account with online statements, many of the transactions will already be marked, and all you have to do is review them for accuracy.

4. As you mark transactions, Quicken updates its balance to the ending balance shown on your statement, and displays the difference between them. With Quicken to do your calculations for you, this process goes quickly and accurately. When all the transactions on your statement are marked as cleared, Quicken and your bank balance should agree—you have completed reconciling. If the numbers don't match, you can correct the mistakes or take other appropriate steps.

80

When you've completed reconciling, Quicken marks all the reconciled transactions with an **R** in the Clr column of the register. This means they've been reconciled and they won't appear in future reconciliation sessions.

Now that you have the basic idea of how to reconcile your account, let's look further at the details. For this chapter, I'll assume that you've begun entering your own 'real' checks into the register, that you're working with your last bank statement, and that you've "turned on" online banking.

Balancing Your Account the First Time

When you begin to work with Quicken, it's common to find discrepancies between your bank statement and your Quicken account. That's because the two records contain different sets of transactions.

The bank statement reflects only the transactions that have been posted to your account. These include cashed checks, but not the checks you've already sent that haven't yet been cashed. Your Quicken records contain *all* the checks you've written, whether or not they have been cashed. But they don't include items generated by the bank such as interest payments and service charges.

For this reason, you shouldn't be surprised if you have trouble finding exact agreement between the bank and Quicken the first time you balance. You'll learn techniques for handling these problems later in this chapter. But there are some steps you can take now, before you try to reconcile the first time, that can minimize the difficulty:

1. *Be sure the opening balance for the account matches the closing balance on your last bank statement.* The first key to successfully reconciling your Quicken account with the bank statement is to start from the same place the bank does. When you set up your first Quicken account you should have used the closing balance from your last bank statement as the new account's initial balance. If you did, you're in good shape. If not, it's time to find the old statement. Find the opening balance transaction in the Quicken register and change the amount to match the closing balance on the statement.

NOTE

Feel free to ignore this sage advice and use another figure as your opening balance—you can still reconcile successfully, if not as quickly. See the section "Dealing with Balancing Problems" later in this chapter.

2. *Enter any missing transactions in your Quicken register, copying them from your current bank statement.* Quicken can do this for you if you update your account via your online statement—you learned how earlier in this chapter. To do it by hand, scan the current paper statement looking for transactions that aren't yet in your Quicken register. Most likely, these would be checks you wrote in a previous month. If you find any, enter them in the register before you start to reconcile.

3. *Enter any other transactions that are not reflected in any of your bank statements to date.* If you know of earlier checks that are still outstanding as of the current statement, enter them in the register. Eventually, they will clear the bank and show up on a new statement. (Although it will be less confusing if you enter them now, you can enter missing transactions as you reconcile, too.)

Beginning the Balancing Process

Even if you're reconciling against your paper bank statement, you'll save time if you retrieve your latest bank statement first via online banking. That way, Quicken will see to it that all transactions that have cleared your bank are recorded in your register, in case you forgot to enter some. And it will check off all cleared transactions for you, leaving you with less to do during reconciliation.

Begin from the register for the account you want to balance. When you switch to the register, check that the correct account is displayed—the account name is always listed in large type at the top of the register. If not, click the button for the right one in the account selector just below the main section of the register.

Now follow these steps:

82

1. Click the **Reconcile** button on the Iconbar, shown here:

    Quicken displays a small box (Figure 4.6), asking if you're reconciling against your current paper statement or an online statement.

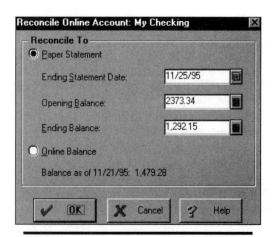

Figure 4.6 Begin reconciling with this box.

2. Click the button for the reconciliation method you've chosen (paper or online). If you're reconciling against your paper statement, you should also review the related fields:

   • Change the date at Ending Statement date to match the date on the statement.

   • The amount Quicken has calculated as the Opening Balance should match the statement's opening balance. If not, correct it to match the opening balance on your statement (you'll be asked for additional information later to account for this discrepancy).

NOTE

The first time you balance, the Opening Balance field lists the balance that you entered when you first created your Quicken account. From then on, the amount Quicken calculates for the Opening Balance is the total of all reconciled transactions in your account.

   • Fill out the Ending Balance field. Here, copy the ending balance amount from the statement (it may also be listed as the new balance or the closing balance).

3. Click **OK** to proceed to the Reconcile Bank Statement window—the reconciliation window, for short—shown in Figure 4.7.

   If you've chosen to reconcile to your online statement, Quicken first goes online, retrieving your current online statement. If the statement contains transactions that are missing from your register, Quicken displays them in the Update Register window where you can review and correct them as detailed earlier in this chapter. Click **Reconcile** to display the Reconcile Bank Statement window. If you don't have new transactions, or if you're balancing against a paper statement, the Reconcile Bank Statement window comes up automatically (see Figure 4.7).

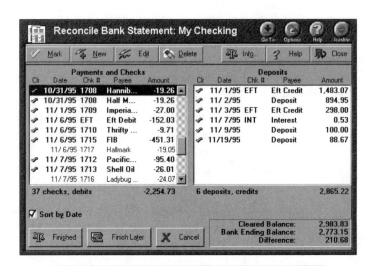

Figure 4.7 The Reconcile Bank Statement window.

4. Now comes the actual reconciling process. Your job is to tick off the items shown in the reconciliation window against the cleared items in your statement. The window lists all the transactions in your account that have not yet been reconciled: Checks and other payments are on the left, deposits on the right. To clear a transaction, just click it so that a yellow check mark appears in the left column (click again to remove the mark). If you've updated your register via an online statement, some or all of the transactions may be marked already—just leave them that way.

Use a pen or pencil to check off each item on your bank statement after you've marked it as cleared in the reconciliation window.

TIP

5. When *all* the items appearing on your statement have been marked in the window, the amount labeled *Difference* in the lower-right corner should be zero. When it is, you've successfully balanced your account. Click the **Finished** button. You'll

be given an opportunity to print a reconciliation report, and then you're returned to the register.

Back in the register, you can see that Quicken has marked all the reconciled transactions with an "R" in the Clr column. These transactions will never again show up in the reconciliation window, though they continue to figure in the account balance.

Reconciling with Quicken is a fairly straightforward process, and the instructions above should suffice for many people. But complications arise often enough that some additional information and tips on handling problems are in order—read on if you like.

More about the Reconciliation Window

In the reconciliation window, Quicken displays several totals in the lower-right corner. Here's what each line means:

- The amount labeled *Cleared Balance* is the total of all the transactions in the reconciliation window marked with a yellow check. Each time you clear a transaction, Quicken adds it to this amount. As you clear transactions Quicken also keeps running subtotals of cleared payment and deposit transactions on either side of the window.

- The Bank Ending Balance is the closing balance taken from the bank statement when you started reconciling.

- The "bottom line" is the amount labeled *Difference*, which tells you the difference between the Cleared Balance and the Bank Ending Balance. When this amount is zero, you've successfully balanced your account. If you can't achieve a zero difference, you may need the hints in "Dealing with Balancing Problems," later in this chapter.

- If you had to change the opening balance Quicken had calculated to match the opening balance on your bank statement, the difference between the two amounts appears on an extra line at the lower right, labeled *Opening Balance Difference*. If an opening balance difference is shown, remember that you'll have to account for this discrepancy later. (See "Dealing with Balancing Problems," later in this chapter).

Adding Missing Transactions

Occasionally, you'll need to add transactions to your account as you reconcile. This will be obvious when your statement shows transactions that don't appear in your Quicken account. For example, if you're balancing your account the very first time, or after skipping one or more months, there may be checks you assumed had cleared only now showing up on this month's statement. Or you may have simply neglected to enter a paper check or deposit during the current cycle.

As I've already advised, the easiest and most error-free way to add these missing transactions is by having Quicken update your account for you, before you start reconciling. Just connect to the online banking service, grab your latest online statement, and update the register with any new transactions Quicken finds—the technique is covered in full earlier in this chapter.

If you prefer, however, you may make changes in your register yourself as you reconcile. You can type in missing transactions, or change any transaction that doesn't match what the statement says it should be.

To make these changes, use the button bar at the top of the reconciliation window. Click **New** to switch to the register with a new transaction. To change one of the transactions in the reconciliation window, click the transaction to highlight it, then click the **Edit** button. The register will appear with that transaction selected for editing. When you're through making changes, switch back to the reconciliation window by clicking **Close** in the register. Be sure the new or changed transaction is marked with that yellow check.

But before adding or changing register transactions, be sure you're satisfied that your records are in error and the bank statement is correct. Banks make errors, too.

Dealing with Balancing Problems

When the dust settles and you've finished marking all your cleared transactions, the amount labeled *Difference* should be zero. If it is, you've balanced your account and your work is through.

If not, check for an amount labeled *Opening Balance Difference* just above. If the two amounts are equal, you've successfully balanced your account, but you must still account for the opening balance discrepancy. See "Handling an Opening Balance Difference," later in this chapter. If the amount at Difference isn't zero and *doesn't* match Opening Balance Difference, your account hasn't balanced. See "What to Do when You Can't Balance," later in this chapter.

Handling an Opening Balance Difference

If there is a difference between the amount Quicken calculated as your opening balance and the opening balance listed on your bank statement, you must eventually account for the gap. Short of a bank error, there are two situations in which Quicken's opening balance and the one on your bank statement will conflict:

- You are balancing your account for the first time. Earlier, I recommended that you correct the amount of the opening balance transaction in your register to match the opening balance shown on your statement. If you didn't take that step, the opening balance discrepancy persisted during reconciliation. The easy way out: from the reconciliation window, click **Edit** to return to the register, find the opening balance transaction, and fix the amount.

- You are balancing your account with your most recent bank statement after you skipped reconciling for one or more months. In this case, the problem is extra uncleared transactions in the register, assuming you've been using Quicken regularly to record your checks and deposits. Your account now contains a number of transactions that have cleared your bank on previous statements but that are not marked as reconciled in Quicken. To maintain accurate records, it's best to go back and reconcile consecutively every month you missed, then reconcile this month's statement. A second-best approach is to forego full reconciliation and just manually mark off in the register all transactions that appeared on earlier bank statements—type an **R** in the Clr column to do so. And if you don't want to go even that far, just click the **Adjust** button when Quicken offers to create a special balance adjustment transaction when you conclude the balancing process. From now on, at least, you should be in sync with the bank.

What to Do When You Can't Balance

If the amount at Difference in the Reconciliation window is anything other than zero, and if it doesn't equal the amount at Opening Balance Difference, either you or the bank has made an error. There are two common reasons for a discrepancy:

- You've marked the wrong number of payments or deposits as cleared; or

- At least one of the transaction amounts in your Quicken account doesn't match the corresponding items on your statement.

And you have two ways to deal with the problem:

- The preferred approach is to find and correct the transactions on which your register and your statement don't agree; but

- You can decide to have Quicken adjust its own balance arbitrarily to match the one on your statement—dangerous, unless the difference is tiny, but at least this brings you into balance for the future.

To take the easy way out, just click **Finish** and accept Quicken's offer to create a special adjustment transaction for you. But if you're willing to trace the source of the problem, you can take methodical steps to locate it as quickly as possible.

Your bank statement should list separately the number of cleared debit and credit transactions and their totals. Compare each of these values in turn to those in the reconciliation window in Quicken. If the number of, say, debit items doesn't match, you've probably just cleared one too many of the checks or payment transactions, or failed to clear one of them (or perhaps it's still missing from your account). If the number of items match but the totals diverge, you or the bank may have recorded one or more transactions with the wrong amount.

Keep searching until you identify the problem. If it's your mistake, clear or unclear the correct transactions, or switch to the register (click **Edit** or **New**) and make the necessary additions or changes.

If it appears the bank has made the error, things get more complicated. So that you can balance correctly now, create a new transaction in the amount of the error (click **New** to do this), giving it a payee entry such as **Bank Error Adjustment**. Now you can complete the balancing process.

Next, report the problem to your bank's customer service department—you can use online banking mail to do this (see "Exchanging Mail with Your Bank" later in this chapter). Assuming the bank agrees with your bookkeeping, you'll see the necessary adjustment in your account on your next statement. You'll need to create another special transaction in your register for the bank's adjustment—or let Quicken create the transaction for you, via a register update from your online bank statement.

Interrupting the Balancing Process

Don't worry if something comes up that forces you to leave Quicken before completing the balancing process. Just click **Finish Later** in the reconciliation window. You'll be returned to the register. There, any transactions you marked as cleared will be listed with a "c" in the Clr column. When you resume reconciling—just repeat the steps given earlier—those transactions will still be marked in the reconciliation window. Just remember—don't make any changes in the Clr field except while you're reconciling.

Exchanging Mail with Your Bank

Quicken lets you exchange "electronic mail" with your bank or other financial institution. You can write to your bank to ask about services or charges pertaining to your accounts, to make suggestions or lodge complaints, or to ask for help with a specific problem such as a balancing error. Your bank's customer service staff will respond within a day or two, delivering the reply via your online banking service. The bank may sometimes send messages about their services or special offers as well.

To prepare a message for the bank, follow these steps:

1. Display the Online Banking window by opening the Online menu and choosing **Online Banking**.

2. Click the **Mail** button. Quicken displays the window shown in Figure 4.8.

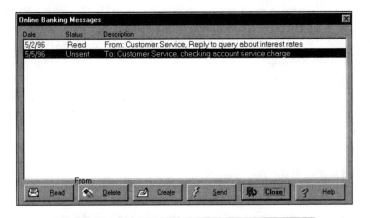

Figure 4.8 Use this window to access electronic mail services in Quicken.

3. Click the **Create** button. You'll now see the window in which you actually type your message (Figure 4.9).

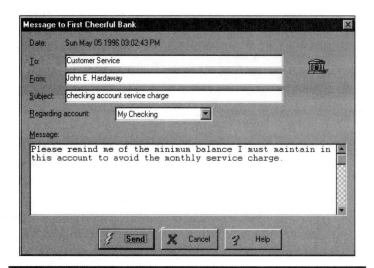

Figure 4.9 Enter your online message to your bank in this window.

4. In the fields at the top of the window type in your name and a brief synopsis of the subject of your message. Use the large area below to compose the message itself.

5. When the message is complete, click **Send**. Quicken goes online and delivers the message.

Quicken "picks up" electronic mail addressed to you every time you connect to the online banking service to retrieve an online statement. If you've received any mail, you'll see a message to that effect in the Transmission Summary window Quicken displays after connecting to the service.

NOTE

Be aware that there's no separate command for checking for mail. When you connect to the online banking service, you'll always receive the current bank statement.

When you return to the Online Banking window, click the **Mail** button. Quicken displays a list of your incoming messages. Double-click on the one you want to read, and it appears in a separate window.

Summary

Online banking is a genuine improvement on older technologies when it comes to interacting with your bank. You get the information you need to make good financial decisions sooner and more accurately with an online statement. And you can control the earning power of your funds by moving them from account to account as your needs dictate. Of course, you still have to balance your accounts regularly, but online bank statements and Quicken's easy reconciling process take the drudgery out of balancing. In the next chapter, you'll learn how online bill payment complements online banking to further streamline everyday financial chores.

CHAPTER FIVE:

Paying Bills Online

Being able to pay your bills online means freedom—freedom from writing and signing checks and from stuffing, licking, and stamping envelopes. More importantly, it means you can pay all your bills for an entire month or more in a single sitting and still keep the money in your account right up until each bill's due date. By combining online bill payment with the online banking methods covered in the last chapter, you take full advantage of Quicken's power.

This chapter covers all the basic techniques you'll need to know to create, send, and track individual online payments. In Chapter 6, you'll build on the skills you master here, learning powerful methods for paying all your monthly bills and other recurring payments automatically.

A Review of Online Payment Basics

If you worked through Chapters 2 and 3, you're already acquainted with the basic method for making and sending online payments. For easy reference, though, this chapter opens with a quick summary of the steps involved.

Setting up for Online Bill Payment

Here's an outline of the steps required to prepare for paying bills online:

1. *Set up your modem in Quicken.* If your modem isn't already set up, open the Online menu and choose **Set Up Modem**.

2. *Obtain an Intuit membership.* If you don't already have an Intuit membership, open the Online menu and choose **Intuit Membership —> Set Up**.

3. *Arrange with your bank to activate online bill payment.* If you have more than one account, you must activate separately each account you'll be using to pay bills online. If your bank doesn't offer online bill payment, you can sign up for it directly with Intuit Servies Corporation at (708) 585-8500—the service is available for checking accounts at any U.S. financial institution.

4. *In Quicken, activate the corresponding account for online payment.* In the Account List window, find the Quicken checking account representing the bank account you'll be using for online payments. Edit the account setup so that the box labeled **Enable Online Bill Payment** is checked. If you don't already have a Quicken account for this bank account, create one, making sure you've enabled online bill payment.

5. *Obtain the list of payees your bank can pay electronically.* Open the Online menu and choose **Online Bill Payment**. Then, with your modem ready, click **Send**. When Quicken connects with the online banking center your computer receives the list of these "standard" payees.

6. *Set up your own online payees.* The bank will pay them by printing and mailing a paper check. Open the Lists menu and choose **Online Payees** to display the Online Payee List window. For each individual or business to which you plan to send online payments, click **New**, then enter the payee's name and address, your account number with that payee, and the payee's phone number. (You can also set up your own online payees as you enter online payments.)

Creating Online Payments

In Chapter 3, you had a chance to practice making an online payment with the sample Quicken check you wrote to the JumboGiant superstore. You can refer back to that discussion for detailed coverage of the procedures involved in filling out a Quicken check.

However, you should know that you can create online payments in the register as well as in the Write Checks window. It doesn't matter which method you use—the resulting payments are identical.

Writing a Check for an Online Payment

Here's a summary of the steps required to write an online check:

1. Switch to the Write Checks window (click the **Go To** button and choose **Write Checks**).

2. If you have more than one account, be sure the active account is the one you want to use for this payment. If not, click the button at the bottom of the check for the correct account (again, the account must already have been set up for online bill payment).

3. Just below the screen check, be sure the box labeled **Online Payment** is checked. If not, click it to add the check mark.

4. Fill out the check. In the *Date* field, Quicken has entered **ASAP** (see Figure 5.1), meaning that it will calculate the earliest possible date the check will be paid based on the payee. You can enter a specific later date if you like (see "Dating Online Payments" later in this chapter). In the *Payee* field, choose from the list of existing online payees or type in a payee name. In the latter case, you'll have to set up the payee for online bill payment as soon as you move out of the *Payee* field. If you haven't changed the date, Quicken sets the date for you based on the payee you've selected as soon as you complete the *Payee* field.

5. Complete the check by filling out the *Amount, Category* and *Memo* fields.

6. Click **Record** to add the check transaction to your account.

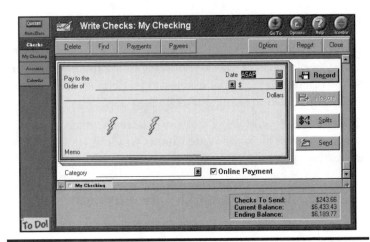

Figure 5.1 Notice how Quicken enters **ASAP** as the date of a new online payment. As soon as you select a payee, Quicken calculates the earliest possible date the payment can arrive.

96

Creating Online Payments in the Register

If you prefer to enter online payments in the register, here's the technique:

1. Switch to the register for the account you're using for online bill payment.

2. Highlight the first empty transaction at the bottom of the register.

3. Skip over the **Date** field if you want Quicken to calculate the earliest possible date the payment will be made. Otherwise, type in a date yourself (see "Dating Online Payments" later in this chapter).

4. Enter **Send** in the *Num* field (type the entry or choose it from the list). This tells Quicken you're working on an online payment. See Figure 5.2.

5. Press **Tab** to move to the *Payee* field. Make an entry here from the list of available online payees or type in a new payee name. If you enter a new payee, Quicken will ask you to set up the

payee for online payment as soon as you move to the next field.

6. Fill out the *Payment, Category,* and *Memo* fields.

7. Click **Record** to add the completed transaction to your account.

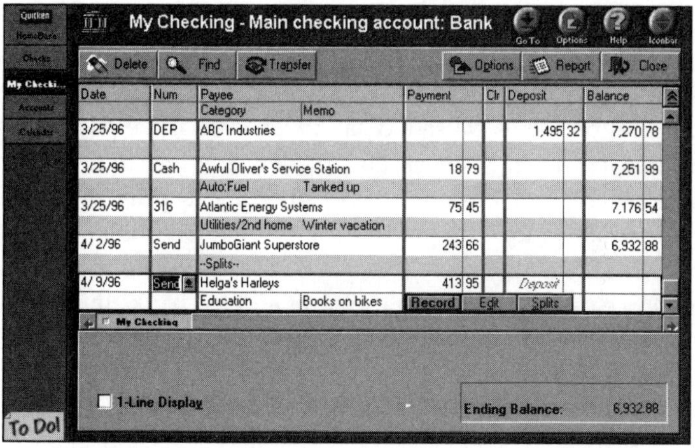

Figure 5.2 Entering an online payment in the register.

Once you've sent the payment request (see "Sending Online Payments" below), Quicken places a check number assigned by the online payment service along with a little lightning bolt in the *Num* field.

| 4/12/96 | 102 ⚡ | Nordstrom | Clothing | | 55 25 |

Dating Your Online Payments

Understanding how to date online bill payments is key to controlling your cash flow and avoiding late payments. The basic idea is this: the date of an online payment tells your bank when the payee should actually receive the payment. In other words, it's *not* the date your bank is supposed to send the payment to the payee.

This system is the easiest possible approach to dating online payments, as you'll see in a moment. It does mean you have to get used to putting the date you want the payment to arrive on the screen check, rather than today's date.

There's a simple reason the payment date works this way: It's because the *lead time* for online payments varies from payee to payee. Lead time is the interval between the processing date, when the bank "cuts the check," and the date the payee receives the payment. You can see the lead time for each payee in the Online Payee list.

For payees the bank pays electronically, the lead time is usually just one business day (although electronic fund transfers are instantaneous, the bank builds in a one-day cushion just in case high volume or technical problems cause a delay). However, if the payment must be printed on a paper check and mailed, the lead time is usually assumed to be four business days—one day to print and mail the check, three days for it to get there. (You may be dubious about the Postal Service's ability to deliver payments anywhere in the country within three days, but apparently Intuit and the banks think it can be done.)

Now suppose every time you created an online payment you had to look up the lead time for each payee, subtract that from the date you want the payment to arrive, and then adjust the answer to account for weekends and holidays. The potential for errors would be high, and anyway, this is the kind of tedious work computers were meant to do.

Entering a Date When You Create Online Payments

With this background information in mind, it's easy to decide what date to enter when you create an online payment. Here are the two simple scenarios to consider:

> *You want the payment to arrive as soon as possible.* In this case, you don't have much to do. If you're filling out an online check in the Write Checks window, leave Quicken's automatic entry of **ASAP** in the *Date* field. If you're filling out a register transaction, just set the date to today's date if some other date is showing. When you record the transaction, Quicken will change the date to the earliest possible one.

You want the payment to arrive on a specific date. This one is easy, too. Change the date to the date you want the recipient to *receive* the payment. Of course, this has to be a date later than the one Quicken automatically enters for the as-soon-as-possible payments. And to be safe, you should select a date a few days before the bill is actually due. That gives you a little fudge factor in case the payee doesn't post payments every day.

Sending Online Payments

In the next few sections, you'll learn all about using the Online Bill Payment window to send payments and handle other related chores. But the basic method for sending in an online payment—actually, an online payment *instruction*—is simple. You open the Online Bill Payment window and click **Send**. Everything else is done for you.

Although you can send individual online payments at any time, it's simpler to send a whole batch all at once. You can create a number of online payments all at once or on different days, then send them all in at once when it's convenient to go online.

Going Online with the Online Bill Payment Window

The Online Bill Payment window is your access point for online bill payment services. Display the window, shown in Figure 5.3, by opening the Online menu and choosing **Online Bill Payment**.

The key to all online action with the Online Bill Payment window is the **Send** button at the lower right. Although the button is labeled *Send*, its basic function is to take you online, connecting you to the online bill payment service. Even if you don't have payments to make at the time, you can use the **Send** button to access payment records and exchange messages with the service.

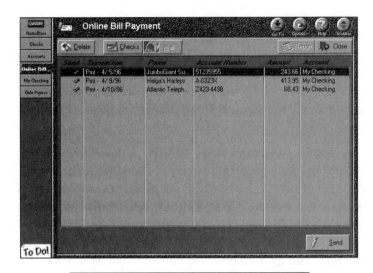

Figure 5.3 The Online Bill Payment window.

For example, if you simply want to find out whether a check has actually been sent yet, you can go online with the **Send** button to transmit a payment inquiry to the online payment service. And whenever you go online, whether or not you have payments to send, any modifications you've made to your online payee list are transmitted to the service.

In fact, before you even begin creating online payments, you should connect to the service at least once to obtain the list of the payees your bank can pay electronically, rather than with a mailed check. Just open the Online Bill Payment window and click **Send**—your online payee list will be updated automatically.

Sending Payments with the Online Bill Payment Window

Most of the Online Bill Payment window is devoted to a list of the online payments you've created but haven't yet sent. For each payment, the list displays a description of the transaction, the payee name and account number, the payment amount, and the account it will come from.

In the Send column at the far left, Quicken displays a key bit of information: whether or not to send the payment when you connect to the online bill payment service. If you see a yellow check mark in the Send column, as shown here:

the payment will be sent. If the check mark is absent, Quicken holds on to the payment until you give the word.

When you're ready to send in one or more payments, here's how to proceed:

1. Review the list. If you spot a payment you don't want to send yet, just click over the payment to remove the check mark in the Send column. To restore the check mark to payments you previously unmarked, click the transaction again.

TIP

If you want to modify a payment before sending it, *double-click* the item in the list (click twice quickly). Quicken displays the transaction in your register, where you can make and record any changes you wish. Then click **Close** to return to the Online Bill Payment window.

2. Click **Send**. Quicken activates your modem, connecting you to the online bill payment service. Once a connection is made, Quicken transfers your payment instructions to the service.

3. After the payments are sent, Quicken displays a report on the number of transactions you sent and their amount (Figure 5.4). Any problems that occurred with the transmission are reported as well.

Once you've sent an online payment, Quicken removes it from the list in the Online Bill Payment window. The payment is still listed in your register, of course. In the next section, you'll learn how to track online payments in the register as well as with the Online Bill Payment window.

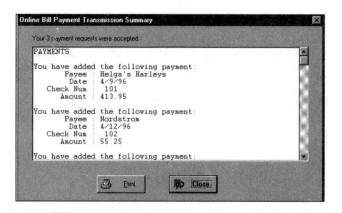

Figure 5.4 In this window, Quicken summarizes the payments you sent and any messages exchanged between you and the online payment service.

Recordkeeping for Online Bill Payment

As you know, online payments are recorded like any other transactions in your register. As soon as you record an online payment, and even before you send it to the online bill payment service, Quicken subtracts the payment amount from the account balance. That way, you always know how much money you have left to work with in your account, even though the bank's balance won't show the online payment until it is processed.

Finding and Examining Online Payments in the Register

You learned earlier that online payments you haven't yet sent are listed in the register with the entry **Send** in the *Num* field. To locate these not-yet-sent online payments in your register quickly, use the **Find** command:

1. Click the **Find** button on the register's toolbar. You'll be filling out the Find window as shown in Figure 5.5.

Figure 5.5 The Find window completed as you would do to locate unsent online payments.

2. Begin by skipping to the *Search* field where you should choose **Check number** (corresponding to the *Num* field in the register) in the drop-down list.

3. Now move back to the *Search* field. The drop-down list here now offers only options relevant to the *Num* field. From these, choose **Send**.

4. Leave the *Match* if field set to **Contains**.

5. Click **Find** to locate the next unsent online payment in the register. You can keep clicking **Find** to view all the payments in turn or until you find the particular payment you're looking for.

You can't use the **Find** command to locate online payments that have already been sent. But they're easy to spot visually. In addition to the "check number" assigned by the online payment service, the *Num* field for each sent online payment displays a small but bright yellow lightning bolt.

Requesting Information Online about a Payment

To follow up on the status of an online payment you've already sent, use the payment inquiry function. You might want to do this for extremely important payments when you want to ensure that the bank has actually sent the payment.

To initiate a payment inquiry:

1. Find and highlight the payment transaction in the register.

2. Open the Edit menu and choose **Payment Inquiry**. A small window appears listing the details Quicken currently has on file (Figure 5.6). Leave the **Update Status** button selected (the section on sending and receiving messages below tells you how to use the other button, labeled **Create Message**).

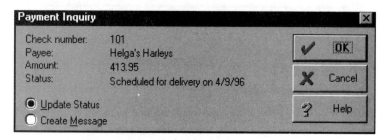

Figure 5.6 The Payment Inquiry window.

3. Click **OK** to go online. When Quicken connects to the online service, the transaction details will be updated and displayed.

4. Review the message you receive. If you get a message such as "There is an error with this payment" you should call the online bill payment service at (708) 585-8500.

Of course, the only way to know for sure if the payee has deposited your money is to check the bank statement for the account from which the funds were sent. With online banking, you can get this information as soon as the bank posts it, without having to wait for your monthly paper statement or placing a telephone call.

Recording the Online Bill Payment Service Charge

Although many banks are offering a free trial period for online bill payment, you'll eventually be charged a monthly fee for this service. Since this fee will appear on your bank statement each month, you won't have to record it manually if you bank online (see Chapter 4). If you don't use online banking, however, be sure to record the service charge, either by adding it to any other banking fees you pay and listing the total in the *Service Charge* field when you reconcile or by entering the fee as a separate payment transaction in the register. If you take the latter approach, you can schedule the transaction for automatic entry each month (see Chapter 6).

Stopping and Changing Online Payments

Once you've sent a payment to the online payment service, you can cancel it right up until its *processing date*—the date on which the bank prepares the payment. Quicken won't let you proceed if the processing date has passed. You may still be able to stop payment on a check by calling the bank.

As long as the processing date hasn't yet arrived, you can change a pending online payment by first canceling it and then sending the new version of the payment. To make things less confusing, it's probably best not to create the new payment until after you stop the first payment.

NOTE

You can cancel any individual payment in a sequence of online repeating payments, or you can cancel the whole sequence. For details, see Chapter 6.

Here's how to stop a payment with Quicken:

1. Find and highlight the payment transaction you want to stop.

2. Open the Edit menu and choose **Stop Payment**.

3. Quicken displays a box asking if you really want to stop the payment. Click **OK** to proceed, storing the stop payment instruction.

4. Open the Online menu and choose **Online Bill Payment**. When the window appears, click the **Send** button. Quicken dials the online bill payment service, sending in your stop payment order.

Note that Quicken doesn't delete stopped payments from the register. Instead, it marks them with a little stop sign icon in the Num column, and adds the notation **VOID** to the existing entry in the Payee field, as shown here :

4/ 9/96	101	🛑	Helga's Harleys	Bike supplies	413	95
4/12/96	102	✂	Nordstrom	Clothing	55	25
4/15/96	103	🛑	Shell Oil Company	Auto:Fuel	22	76

This way, you have a record of the transaction, but the payment amount doesn't affect your balance.

106 Sending and Receiving Messages about Your Online Payments

The online bill payment service provides for the times when you need to communicate with your bank about a payment or your account in general.

Sending Messages to the Online Bill Payment Service

When you have questions about a payment that a standard payment inquiry won't answer, or you need information about the online bill payment service or your account, you can write and send in your own messages with Quicken. Here's how:

1. Start as if you were making a standard payment inquiry: highlight the payment in question in the register, open the Edit menu, and choose **Payment Inquiry**.

2. When the Payment Inquiry window appears (Figure 5.6), click the button labeled **Create message**.

3. Quicken expands the Payment Inquiry window as shown in Figure 5.7. Type in your message and your "signature"—your name—in the spaces provided.

4. Click **OK** to go online and send your message.

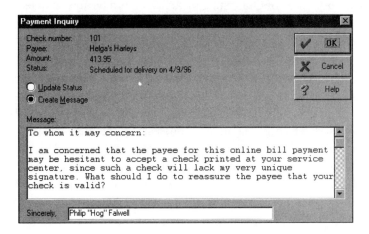

Figure 5.7 Compose your messages to the online payment service in this window.

Receiving Messages

From time to time, the online bill payment service will send you messages about your account and the available services, as well as responses to messages you've sent to it. You don't have to request that such messages be sent—you'll get them automatically each time you go online with the service by clicking the **Send** button in the Online Bill Payment window. If you have sent a message and are expecting a reply, you can do this even if you don't have payments to send in.

If you've received any messages from the service, they will be listed in the Transmission Summary window. Once you return to the Online Bill Payment window, click the **Mail** button. Quicken displays a list of the incoming messages. Click the message you want to read and then click—what else?—the **Read** button.

107

About CheckFree

Previous versions of Quicken let you pay bills electronically with a third-party service called *CheckFree*. If you were using CheckFree with an earlier version of Quicken, Quicken 5 should be able to detect this at installation time. You'll still be able to use CheckFree as before. However, Quicken 5 won't let you set up CheckFree service for the first time.

If you do have an existing CheckFree account, you can switch to Intuit's online bill payment service any time you like. To make the switch, you should be sure that all pending payments have been transmitted to CheckFree, and you must set up for online bill payment as described earlier in this chapter. When you choose **Online Bill Payment** on the Online menu, Quicken asks if you want to disable CheckFree. Click **OK** to confirm the switch. If you want to switch back, open the Activities menu, then choose **CheckFree**.

When you switch to online bill payment from CheckFree, Quicken automatically transfers your CheckFree payees to the online payee list. One detail you'll have to take of yourself is cancelling the CheckFree service: you'll receive a monthly bill until you call CheckFree at 800/297-3180 to discontinue your account.

Summary

In this chapter you learned the methods you'll need to take advantage of online bill payment. In addition to creating and sending the payments themselves, you now know how to track the payments in your account, send stop payment orders, make payment inquiries, and exchange other messages with the online bill payment service. You need to learn only one more major technique to complete your mastery of online bill payment: setting up payments that are executed automatically at regular intervals.

CHAPTER SIX:

Automating Your Records

With Quicken's rudiments under your belt, it's time to learn about some more advanced features that minimize the work you do recording transactions.

In this chapter, we'll cover:

- *memorized transactions*, transactions you can use again and again with a minimum of typing
- *online repeating payments,* payments that you tell your bank to make automatically for you on a repeating basis
- *scheduled transactions*, transactions that Quicken automatically enters in your account at the appropriate time
- *transaction groups,* which let you record entire groups of transactions automatically at scheduled intervals

Using Memorized Transactions

Quicken automatically "memorizes" every register transaction and payment you record, and can instantly recall the information. Once you've made a payment to the water company for your monthly bill,

Quicken lets you reuse all the information from that transaction the next time the bill is due. All you have to do is add the new date and this month's amount, and Quicken does the rest.

As Quicken is normally set up, this memorization feature works automatically on every transaction you record in the register or Write Checks window. You can shut off automatic memorization if you like, but there's rarely a good reason to do so. Quicken shuts off automatic memorization once you accumulate something like 2000 memorized transactions.

If automatic memorization does get shut off, you can still manually memorize individual transactions you expect to need in the future. You can also prune the list of memorized transactions to eliminate the dead wood.

110 Understanding Memorized Transactions

Quicken memorizes and recalls transactions by payee, which stands to reason. As you'll see in the next section, you call on memorized transactions when you're filling out the Payee field in the register or a screen check.

Quicken can only memorize one transaction for each payee. Quicken's "remembers" only the details from the most recently memorized transaction for each payee. Each time a new transaction gets memorized—automatically or manually—Quicken replaces the existing memorized information in the Deposit or Payment, Category, and Memo fields.

This fact can be both a blessing and a slight limitation. The list of memorized transactions would quickly get unwieldy if Quicken memorized separately each transaction you write to the same payee. On the other hand, if you routinely make or receive payments of different fixed amounts to or from the same payee, separate memorized transactions for that payee would be in order. You can get around this problem by making a slight change in the payee name for each transaction you want to memorize.

Another point to remember is that Quicken automatically memorizes an individual transaction only the *first time* you record it. If you go back and edit the same transaction in the register, any changes you make are not reflected in the memorized version of the transaction unless you re-memorize it manually.

Using Memorized Transactions

Reusing a memorized transaction is a piece of cake. When you reach the Payee field while working on a transaction, Quicken pops up the list of all previously memorized transactions. Just click on the payee you're reusing and Quicken inserts the memorized transaction information in your new transaction. If any of the information needs changing—say the dollar amount or the category entry—just move to the relevant field and type in the new entry.

If you're a decent typist, an even faster technique is to rely on QuickFill. Just as in the Category field, all you do is start typing the payee's name. As soon as Quicken finds a match—usually just one or two letters will do—the program pops in the rest of the information from the matching memorized transaction.

Managing the Memorized Transaction List

There's no point in clogging up your memorized transaction list with lots of transactions you're unlikely to use again—especially when it's so easy to prevent that from happening. There are two ways to do this:

- *Turn off automatic transaction memorization.* If you're pretty sure you've already memorized most of the transactions you'll be using regularly, just turn off automatic memorization of new transactions. Begin by clicking the **Options** button, then the **Register** button. At the top of the Register Options window click the **QuickFill** tab to display the panel shown in Figure 6.1. Click the top option box labeled **Automatic Memorization of New Transactions** so the check mark disappears, then click **OK**.

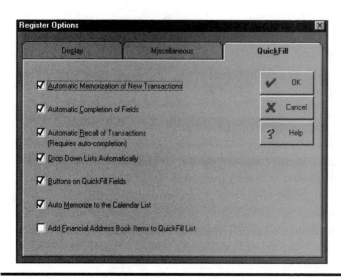

Figure 6.1 The QuickFill panel in the Register Options window.

- *Have Quicken automatically delete memorized transactions you haven't recently used.* Here's a more sophisticated approach to preventing overgrowth of your memorized transaction list: Have Quicken scan your memorized transaction list every time you use the program, deleting any memorized transactions you haven't used in the last, say, 6 months. To activate this watchdog feature, click the **Options** button, then the **General** button. In the General Options window, click the box labeled **Remove Memorized Transactions Not Used in Last** so that it contains a check mark. Then over to the right, enter the number of months for the automatic cutoff.

You can also prune the memorized transaction list selectively. To display the list, open the Lists menu and choose **Memorized Transactions**. You'll see the window shown in Figure 6.2.

To eliminate a transaction, click the transaction in the list then click **Delete**. When you **OK** the confirmatory message, the memorized transaction is gone for good. You can also make changes in any memorized transaction by clicking it in the list and clicking the **Edit** button.

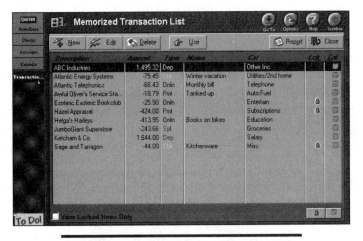

Figure 6.2 The Memorized Transactions List.

113

Memorizing Transactions Manually

If automatic memorization of transactions has been turned off, you can still memorize individual transactions as the need dictates. The easy way: after you've entered a new transaction, press **Ctrl-M**. Quicken lets you confirm the action, then places the transaction in the list.

You can also add memorized transactions in the Memorized Transaction List window (see Figure 6.2). Just click the **New** button and fill out the various fields in the Create Memorized Transaction window. Note that you can memorize Split transaction details by clicking the **Splits** button. You can also memorize the payee address by clicking the **Address** button, but only for printed check transactions.

Locking and Unlocking Memorized Transactions

Normally, each time you record a new transaction for a given payee, Quicken replaces the existing information—the amount, category, and memo entries—with that from the new transaction. This keeps the memorized transaction list current.

Sometimes, however, you'll want to *lock* a memorized transaction to prevent this automatic update. This is useful if you frequently record new transactions with the same transaction information, but occasionally record transactions with different information.

Take the example of the entry you might record for your paycheck deposit every other week. If you usually deposit the same amount for the same 80 hours of work, you'd want to lock the corresponding memorized transaction. That way, recording a deposit for the occasional period you work overtime won't change the memorized transaction.

To lock a memorized transaction, use the Memorized Transaction List window. Open the Lists menu, then choose **Memorized Transactions** to display the window shown in Figure 6.2. Click in the column labeled *Lck* over the row for the transaction you want to lock. A tiny image of a padlock appears to indicate the transaction is locked.

And the last column in the Memorized Transaction List window, the one labeled *Cal*, indicates whether the transaction appears in the list displayed with the Financial Calendar. You'll learn to use the Calendar later in this chapter.

Paying Regular Bills with Online Repeating Payments

Memorized transactions are fine as far as they go, but Quicken can do much more to minimize the work you do in recording payments and deposits. Like most people, you probably pay the same bills and make the same deposits month after month. You may have a car payment or a loan on your new kitchen cabinets, and there's always your rent or mortgage and utility bills. On the income side, there's that regular paycheck to account for. Why not let Quicken handle these regular transactions for you?

It's important to understand that you have two ways to make recurring online payments more or less automatically. Here are your options, and the differences between them:

- *Online repeating payments*—Use online repeating payments for any bill whose amount stays the same each month. That would include your rent or mortgage payment, payments on most other loans, and charges for services like your cable TV subscription. When you set up an online repeating payment, Quicken instructs your bank to make these payments for you at the interval you specify, and for as long as you authorize them. The bank will keep making these payments according to your instructions whether or not you ever again connect with the online bill paying service.

- *Scheduled payments*—Schedule online payments (you'll learn how in the next section) for any bills whose amount varies from month to month, such as your telephone or utility service. When you schedule online payments with the Financial Calendar, Quicken must transmit the payment order to your bank each time the payment is due. This is less convenient, since you have to be sure to connect with the online bill paying service to translate the payment instruction before the bill is due.

Unfortunately, Quicken isn't consistent about the use of these terms, which can be confusing. In some parts of the program, online repeating payments are referred to as entirely separate from scheduled transactions; we'll use that definition here, since you can't create online repeating payments with the scheduled transaction functions in the Financial Calendar. In the Scheduled Transactions List window, however, Quicken includes both types of items, suggesting that online repeating payments are a type of scheduled transaction. Accept the inconsistency or ignore the nomenclature, and follow the instructions in this chapter for working with either type of recurring transaction.

115

TIP

Quicken can automate the accounting process for your loans, linking them to the corresponding online repeating payments. For that matter, it can handle loans you pay with regular checks, too. See Chapter 8.

Setting up Online Repeating Payments

To set up an online repeating payment, begin by displaying the Scheduled Transaction List (unfortunately, Quicken doesn't let you schedule online repeating transactions on the Financial Calendar, covered in the next section). To view the list, open the Lists menu and choose **Scheduled Transactions**. Figure 6.3 shows what you'll see.

116

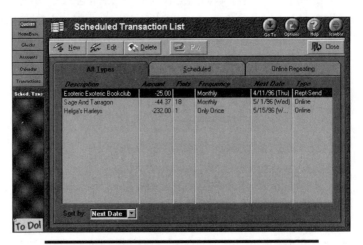

Figure 6.3 The Scheduled Transaction List window.

Now, to create an online repeating payment, follow these steps:

1. Click the **New** button. The Scheduled Transaction Type box, shown in Figure 6.4, appears.

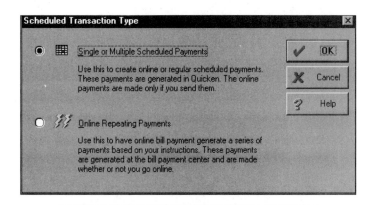

Figure 6.4 The Scheduled Transaction Type box.

2. Here, click the obvious choice: the button labeled **Online Repeating Payments**. Then click **OK**. Quicken now lets you get down to business, displaying the Create Online Repeating Payment window, shown in Figure 6.5.

 117

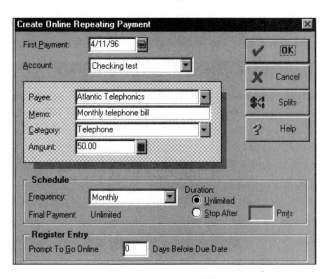

Figure 6.5 The Create Online Repeating Payment window.

3. Fill out the fields in this window as follows:

- *First Payment*—enter the date you want the bank to make the first in the sequence of repeating payments.

- *Account*—choose the account from which the payment should be made. Only the accounts you've activated for online bill payment are available in the drop-down list; if you have only one such account, there's nothing to do here.

- *Payee*—Choose the name of the correct online payee from the drop-down list, or type in a new payee name (in the latter case, Quicken will ask you to set up the new payee when you move out of this field).

- *Memo, Category,* and *Amount*—These fields work just like the corresponding ones in the register. If you want to split the payment over two or more categories, click the **Splits** button.

- *Frequency*—Choose the interval at which you want the bank to make your payment. The available options range from every two weeks to yearly.

- *Duration*—Indicate how long you want the payments to be made. For bills you'll be paying more or less forever, such as bills for monthly services, click the **Unlimited** button. For loan payments and other bills that you expect to stop paying after a specific number of payments, click the **Stop After** button instead, then type in the number of payments left to go. For example, if you've already made 15 payments on a 5-year new car loan, you'd enter **45** in the field labeled *Pmts*.

- *Final payment*—Nothing to do here, since Quicken figures out the date of your final payment based on the settings in the First Payment, Frequency, and Duration fields. But take a close look at the entry Quicken makes to ensure that it gives the actual date you expect to make your final payment. If not, you've probably made an error in one of those earlier fields.

- *Prompt To Go Online*—Your entry here tells Quicken when to remind you to connect to the online banking service center. The reason to connect isn't to tell the bank to make the pay-

118

ment—the bank will do that automatically. Instead, you connect to retrieve the bank's record of the pending automatic payment. Quicken places it into your register so your balance reflects the payment. If you go online to retrieve the payment information at least several days before the payment is actually made, you have time to review it so you can still cancel or alter it if need be.

4. Click **OK** to finish setting up the online repeating payment. Quicken returns you to the Scheduled Transaction List window with the new repeating payment highlighted in the list. Notice the entry in the Type column, **Rept-Send**. *Rept* indicates an online repeating payment, while *Send* means you still have to connect to the online center to send in the payment instruction.

NOTE

Notice that the tabs at the top of the Scheduled Transaction List window let you choose whether to display all types of recurring transactions, only scheduled transactions, or only online repeating payments.

5. Your final step is to activate the payment you've just set up by connecting to the online service center. Open the Online menu and choose **Online Bill Payment**. When the Online Bill Payment window appears, click **Send**.

Editing Online Repeating Payments

To make changes in an online repeating payment, highlight the line for the payment in the Scheduled Transactions List and click the **Edit** button. The window that appears is identical to the Create Online Repeating Payment window, except that it has a different title. Make any changes you like and click **OK**.

Whether or not you've already sent in the payment instruction to the online service center, your next step should be to go online and connect to the center to transmit the corrected payment instructions.

Scheduling Transactions for Automatic Entry Using the Financial Calendar

The Financial Calendar gives you an alternative to online repeating payments when you want Quicken to record transactions in your account automatically. With the calendar, you can create *scheduled* transactions that Quicken adds to your account at the proper time each month, or other intervals you specify.

Online repeating payments have their advantages—they're better for making recurring online payments when the payment amount is fixed. But you'll need scheduled transactions to handle online payments where the amount varies from month to month, for payments you make in cash or by paper check, and for all deposits.

The Financial Calendar has other functions as well. It can show you all the transactions in your register so you can visually associate your spending and earning patterns with their occurrence in time. And you can use it to display a graph showing the net balance in all your accounts over time.

TIP

One time you may want to turn off Quicken 5's new Quick Tabs is when you're working with the calendar. With Quick Tabs off, you can enlarge the calendar window to fill all of the work space available in Quicken's window, making it easier to read items listed on the calendar and providing more room for the optional graph.

Still, the calendar's best use is for scheduling transactions. As you can guess if you've read through the previous section, the Scheduled Transaction List window (Figure 6.3) offers an alternative to the calendar for setting up scheduled transactions. Scheduling transactions with the list isn't difficult, but the calendar makes this process a breeze.

NOTE

The techniques discussed in this section let you schedule individual transactions. You should know that Quicken also lets you create *transaction groups*, batches of transactions that it records in one fell swoop. Since transaction groups are even more powerful than individual scheduled transactions, you might want to read the following section on transaction groups before setting up an extensive set of scheduled transactions.

Displaying and Working with the Financial Calendar Window

To see the calendar, click on the **calendar** button on the Iconbar:

or press **Ctrl-K**. Figure 6.6 shows the window you'll see.

121

Figure 6.6 Quicken's Financial Calendar.

The calendar looks much like an ordinary wall calendar, albeit without any pretty pictures to look at. At the very top Quicken displays the current month and year. You click the **Prev** and **Next** buttons on either side to display the previous or next month. To go to a particular date, click over the main date itself. Quicken pops up a little window in which you can enter the date you want to see, and the calendar switches to that date as soon as you click **OK**.

In the calendar itself, the box for today's date appears in light blue ("cyan" in PC jargon). Other days in the current month are white, while days from the previous month or the next month are gray. A light green highlight indicates the day on which you're currently recording or editing transactions. The date itself is displayed in black type for past dates and blue type for today and the remaining days in the month.

Notice that the calendar displays all of the transactions you've entered in your accounts so far, each in the box for the appropriate date. Previously recorded transactions are in black type, while those scheduled for future entry are in blue, although the color difference is very hard to discern, at least on my screen (if you're working through the book in sequence, you won't have any scheduled transactions at this point).

The right side of the calendar window should display a list of all your *memorized* transactions (unmemorized transactions appear on the calendar itself, but not in this list). You use this list to schedule transactions, as you'll see in the next section. Read on for what to do if the list isn't visible.

The other buttons at the top of the calendar work as follows:

- *Note*—lets you leave a message for today's date.
- *View*—lets you choose which of the calendar's optional elements to display. These are the list of memorized transactions and a bar graph displaying the overall balance of all your accounts by date. To display or hide either element, click **View** and select the corresponding menu choice. A check mark appears beside the menu choice when an element is visible, but is not present if the element is hidden.
- *Options*—lets you select which of your accounts to show on the calendar.

- *Close*—closes the calendar.

At the bottom of the calendar window, three buttons let you select which transactions appear in the calendar:

- *Register*—With this button selected, the calendar only displays transactions that have already been recorded.
- *Scheduled*—With this button selected, the calendar only displays transactions that are scheduled for future entry in your records.
- *Show Both*—Select this button to display both previously recorded and scheduled transactions.

Finally, when the list of memorized transactions is visible, the button below it labeled **Manage List** takes you directly to the Memorized Transactions List window (see Figure 6.2 earlier in this chapter).

Scheduling Transactions with the Calendar

You use the calendar's list of memorized transactions to schedule transactions. Again, if you don't see the list, click the **View** button, then choose the menu item **Show Memorized Txns** to display it.

Scheduling a previously memorized transaction for a future date is as easy as dragging the transaction from the list to the calendar and dropping it on the date you want it recorded. All you have to do then is tell Quicken how often you'll be paying the bill (or receiving the income). You can also create scheduled transactions from scratch. Instead of starting with one of the memorized transactions in the list, you just drag the **NEW** entry at the top of the list onto the calendar.

For example, let's say you want to schedule your monthly utility bill for automatic entry in the register. Whether or not you've recorded (and memorized) a utility payment before in Quicken, here's what you do:

1. Be sure the calendar displays the correct month. If the bill next comes due on the first of next month, you'll probably want to record the transaction in the current month to make sure the

funds get there on time. If the bill is due later next month, click the **Next** button to advance the display.

2. Locate the previously memorized utility payment in the list, using the scroll bar to find it if necessary. Or, to create the scheduled transaction from scratch, use the **NEW** item at the top of the list.

3. Drag the chosen transaction (or **NEW**) to the date when you want to schedule the next payment. When you release the mouse button, Quicken displays the New Transaction window (Figure 6.7).

4. Fill out the New Transaction window (details are covered below), click **OK**, and the transaction appears in the calendar.

124

Note that the calendar displays a copy of each scheduled transaction on every date it is scheduled to be entered in your account. If you've scheduled a monthly transaction, clicking the **Next** button at the top of the calendar will quickly show you that the scheduled transaction appears on the calendar each month.

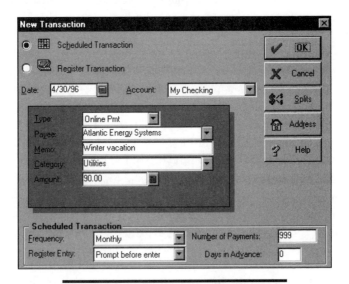

Figure 6.7 The New Transaction window.

Filling out the New Transaction Window

At the very top of the New Transaction window are two buttons, **Scheduled Transaction** and **Register Transaction**. When you drop a transaction (or **NEW**) onto a future date, Quicken automatically selects the **Scheduled Transaction** option. If you accidentally drop the transaction on a *past* date while trying to schedule a transaction for future entry, the **Register Transaction** button will be selected instead. In this case, you should change the setting (and adjust the date for the transaction).

TIP

If you haven't already figured this out, the calendar does more than schedule future transactions—it also provides an alternative to the register for entering past transactions. When you drop a transaction on a past date, the **Register Transaction** button is selected in the New Transaction window. To enter a past transaction, leave this setting as is and fill out the rest of the window with the information called for (it's the same information you'd enter in the register, just organized differently). When you click **OK**, the transaction is recorded in the register.

125

Next comes an area for the date. This specifies the date Quicken should enter this scheduled transaction in your register. If you're scheduling a recurring transaction, Quicken interprets this as the date of the first time the transaction will be recorded.

In the Account field, just to the left of the Date field, select the name of the account where Quicken should record the transaction. To make the selection, use the **Up** and **Down arrow** keys to cycle through the available accounts, or pick from the drop-down list.

Several fields occupy the central portion of the new transaction window. In the Type field, choose the type of the transaction from this selection: **Payment**, **Deposit**, **Print Check**, and **Online Pmt**. Again, use the arrow keys to cycle through the choices or choose from the drop-down list. An entry corresponding to the type you choose will appear in the register's Num column when the transaction is eventually recorded. The rest of the fields here are self-explanatory, corresponding to the same fields in the register.

Scheduling the Transaction

The remaining fields in the New Transaction window appear only if you're creating a scheduled transaction, not recording a register transaction. Here is where you tell Quicken how often to record the transaction and how to handle the process.

In the Frequency field, Quicken has entered **Only Once** for you, meaning a one-time-only scheduled transaction. If you're entering a recurring item, choose the appropriate interval from the drop-down list. The choices are **Weekly, Every two weeks, Twice a month, Every four weeks, Monthly, Every two months, Quarterly, Twice a year,** and **Yearly.**

126

NOTE

There's no "daily" option in the Frequency field for scheduled transactions. Still, rather than enter a daily deposit or payment transaction individually in the register, you can save time by recording a separate scheduled transaction for each working day of the week, choosing the **Weekly** option in the Frequency field.

To the right, the Number of Payments field tells Quicken how many times to enter the transaction into your account. When the entry in the Frequency field is **Only Once**, Quicken automatically sets the Number of Payments field to **1**. The automatic entry for any other frequency is **999**, meaning that Quicken will continue to record transactions until you tell it to stop. That's appropriate for a utility bill, but for a payment on a car loan you would set the Number of Payments field to **36, 48,** or **60.**

Deciding How to Record the Transaction

At the bottom of the New Transaction window, the Register Entry field tells Quicken how to handle the transaction when it comes time to record it. The choices available on the drop-down list are:

- *Automatically enter*, for transactions you're sure you want Quicken to record automatically.

- *Prompt before enter*, for transactions you want to review first. This is useful if the amount of the transaction varies each time you record it, or if there are some periods when you don't record it at all (for example, you may not have a credit card balance every month, and therefore you won't always make a "monthly" credit card payment).

Finally, in the Days in Advance field, enter a number other than 0 if you want Quicken to record the transaction in your account prior to the actual date you chose for the transaction. Quicken will enter the transaction with the original date, but it appears in your account sooner. That way, Quicken will begin reminding you to send the online payment (or print the check) prior to the transaction date.

Scheduling Split Transactions

When you drag a split transaction from the list of memorized transactions to the calendar, Quicken records the split details along with the rest of the information. You can edit this split transaction information—or split a new or previously unsplit transaction—by clicking the **Splits** button in the New Transaction window. The by-now familiar Splits window appears. Use the same techniques you learned in Chapter 3 to add, change, or remove split transaction details, then close the window.

Entering Address Information for Printed Checks

If you're scheduling a check to be printed (rather than an online payment), you can add or edit the payee's address. Click the **Address** button to display a secondary box where you can type in the address information. Then click **OK** to return to the New Transaction window.

Editing Scheduled Transactions

To make changes to a scheduled transaction, highlight its date on the calendar by clicking with the mouse. A tiny window pops up listing all the transactions for that date (Figure 6.8). Highlight the transaction you want to edit and click **Edit**. Quicken displays the Edit Scheduled Transaction window, which is almost identical to the New Transaction window you used to create the scheduled transaction (refer to Figure 6.7 earlier in this chapter).

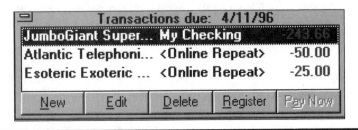

Figure 6.8 Use this window to access scheduled transactions for editing.

Other options available in the window shown in Figure 6.8 include:

- *New*—Clicking here is another way to add a new scheduled or register transaction to the calendar.

- *Delete*—Click this button to remove the transaction from the calendar. Deleting a scheduled transaction in this way doesn't affect any transactions already recorded in the register. However, deleting an already-recorded register transaction from the calendar removes it from the register as well.

- *Pay Now*—Only available when a scheduled transaction or transaction group is selected, this button lets you record a scheduled transaction immediately, no matter when its next scheduled date. Quicken lets you specify the date for the transaction it records in your register, and you can make any other changes you like in the transaction details.

Recording Batches of Items with Transaction Groups

In Quicken, a *transaction group* is a set of transactions that you regularly post to your account at the same time. It's easy to come up with examples of transactions that always occur together—your collection of monthly bills being the obvious one. By collecting these transactions into a transaction group, you can have Quicken record the entire group in a single step.

A transaction group can contain any number of transactions. As you'd expect, you can make modifications after you define the group, add or remove transactions or delete the entire group.

Creating a Transaction Group

Just as with the individual transactions you schedule on the calendar, all the transactions you want to include in a transaction group must be memorized first. That won't be a problem if you've allowed Quicken to memorize all recorded transactions automatically. If not, you can memorize the necessary transactions yourself (see the first section in this chapter for information on memorizing transactions).

The process of creating transaction groups is a little quirky, because you can't create a group directly. Instead, you start by creating a regular scheduled transaction, then transform it into a transaction group. Here are the required steps:

1. In the Financial Calculator, drag the **NEW** item at the top of the calendar's transaction list to the first date you want the group to be recorded. The New Transaction window appears.

2. Fill out a dummy scheduled transaction. Choose a name for the group, something that will readily remind you of its purpose (something like **Monthly bills**), and enter this in the Payee field. In the Account field, choose the account in which you want the group's transactions recorded. The only other required field is Amount, where you can enter any number, even 0. Click **OK** to finalize the entries and return to the calendar.

3. Click on the day containing the dummy scheduled transaction you just created. When Quicken displays the little window listing the transactions for that date (see Figure 6.8), highlight your dummy transaction and click **Edit**. In the Edit Scheduled Transaction window, click the **Groups** button to display the Create New Transaction Group window (Figure 6.9).

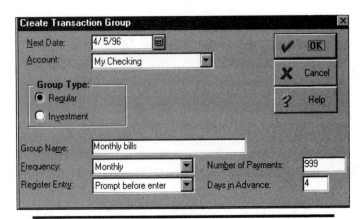

Figure 6.9 The Create New Transaction Group window.

4. Begin defining the actual transaction group in this window. You shouldn't have to change the date, the account into which the group will be recorded, or the group's name, but you can if you like. In the Group Type area, leave the button for **Regular** selected (working with investments is covered in Chapter 9). At the bottom of the window are the key fields that tell Quicken how often to record the transaction group in your account and how to handle the process. These fields work just like those you use to set up individual scheduled transactions (see the previous section).

5. Click **OK**. Quicken next displays a list of all your memorized transactions, like the one shown in Figure 6.10. Here, select transactions to include in the group by double-clicking each transaction (alternatively, you can highlight the transaction and click the **Mark** button at the top left). Transaction groups are assigned numbers by Quicken, and when a transaction is selected for a group, the group number appears in the far right column in the list. To remove a previously selected transaction from the group, repeat the process; the group number entry is cleared, or, if the transaction was previously assigned to another group, that group's number reappears.

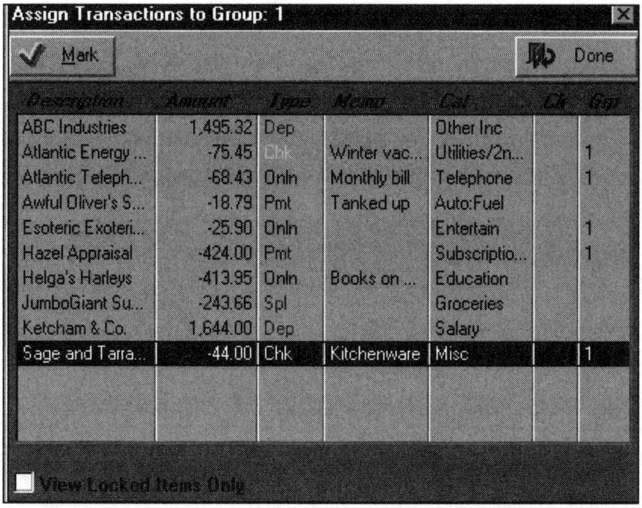

Figure 6.10 The Assign Transactions to Group window.

6. When you're through selecting transactions, click the **Done** button at the top right. You're returned to the calendar. The group appears on the calendar with its numeric designation (Group 1, Group 2, and so forth) followed by a character or two of its name.

Using Transaction Groups

Quicken places the transactions in a group into the account register at the interval you specified when setting up the group. Depending on your choice of options in the Register Entry field when you defined the transaction group, Quicken will give you a chance to approve of the entries first, or make them automatically without further action on your part.

If Quicken is set to "prompt" you before placing the transactions in the register, you'll see a dialog box that lets you change the account in which the group's transactions will be recorded, and the date for each recorded transaction. If you don't want to record the group's transactions at all, click the **Cancel** button in this box.

After a Transaction Group has been Used

After the transactions from a transaction group have been recorded into the register, you're of course free to edit or add to any of the individual transactions that have just been recorded. For example, you may need to change the dollar amounts of one or more transactions.

If the transaction group contained any online payments, don't forget to connect to the online banking service center to send the payment instructions. You should also print any paper check transactions that were included in the group.

Editing and Deleting Transaction Groups

To make changes to a transaction group definition, or to add or subtract individual transactions from the group, begin by locating the group in the calendar. Double-click over the day containing the group to display the little window listing transactions for that date. Locate and highlight the group you want to change and click **Edit** to access the group definition. You can also click **Edit** to delete the group altogether.

Summary

This chapter led you through techniques you'll use regularly to speed your work and sharpen the focus of your Quicken reports and graphs. You should now be fully acquainted with how to use memorized transactions, online repeating payments, scheduled transactions, and transaction groups. In Chapter 7, you'll learn to create customized categories and classes to bring your records into line with your own real-life financial circumstances.

132

CHAPTER SEVEN:

Customizing Your Records with Your Own Categories and Classes

Quicken's set of built-in categories is pretty complete, but odds are good that you'll want to modify it a bit to suit your own situation and taste. You may decide to add categories that fit your own financial situation better, to rename some to your liking, or to remove those you won't be using. And because Quicken doesn't give you any built-in classes, you'll have to create the classes you need from scratch.

Ideally, you should plan a complete list of categories and classes in advance, before you enter any transactions into an account. That way, all your records will be consistent. But for many people, such an organized approach is too much bother. Not to worry—Quicken allows you to add, change, or remove categories and classes any time you please.

Creating New Categories and Classes as You Work

Suppose a friend gets you started on a new hobby—computers, for example. Your spouse is worried about how much all those add-ons and software programs will cost over time, so you agree to keep track. Of course, you know the job will be easy once you create a new Quicken category for your computer-related purchases.

TIP

Some quick advice about creating categories: Short names are best, but only if they're easy to remember. And don't go over-board with large numbers of categories, which can obscure the trends in financial reports and graphs.

You can create the category the first time you record such a purchase in the register. When you get to the Category field, just type in the name you've decided on for your new category. As soon as you move past the Category field, Quicken displays a Set Up Category box (Figure 7.1).

134

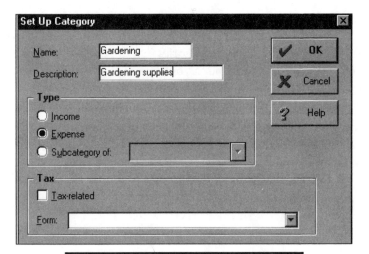

Figure 7.1 The Set Up Category dialog box.

This box lets you enter some basic information about the new category:

- *Description*—Since category names are limited to 15 characters, you're given space to type in a lengthier description of the category.

- *Type*—Based on the type of transaction you're entering, Quicken is usually able to figure out whether you're starting an expense or income category, but you can change the type if you like.

- *Subcategory*—If you're setting up a new subcategory of an existing category, choose the **Subcategory of** button, then select the "parent" category in the list.

- *Tax-related*—Check the **Tax-related** box if the category has anything to do with your taxes. That way, you can prepare reports that cover only tax-related transactions.

- *Form*—Use this field to assign the category to a specific line of the Federal income tax forms. This step is essential if you plan to use Quicken for preparing your tax returns—see "Setting Up Categories and Classes for Income Tax Preparation" later in this chapter. If you don't see the Form field, activate it using the technique described in that section.

WARNING

Be sure you understand this key point: By itself, designating a category as "tax-related" designation is useless in helping you prepare your income tax returns. For that purpose, you must assign the category to a specific line of the tax return in the Form field. See the section below on using categories for income tax preparation.

Once the entries in the Set Up Category box suit you, click **OK** to close the box and create the new category. Quicken places it in your category list with other categories of its kind (income or expense) in alphabetical order.

Adding and Modifying Categories in the Category List Window

When you need to add more than one category, or if you decide to edit or delete one or more existing categories, your ticket is the category list, shown in Figure 7.2. To display it, open the Lists menu and choose **Category and Transfer**.

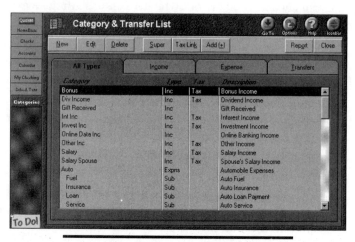

Figure 7.2 The Category and Transfer List.

As you can see, this is a simple list of your categories showing each category's name, type (income or expense), tax-related status, and description. It's just a larger version of the category list you use to enter categories into transactions.

The first column on the left, labeled *Category*, holds the name that Quicken uses when it finds and sorts your transactions by category. To move up and down in the list, scroll with the mouse using the scroll bars, or use the cursor keys on the keyboard (the **Up** and **Down arrow** keys, **PgUp**, **PgDn**, **Home**, and **End** all work). You can also move to a specific category by pressing the first letter of its name, repeatedly if necessary, until the category is highlighted.

The next column, the *Type* column, indicates the type of transaction to be stored there. Income items are labeled *Inc*, expense items are *Expns*, and subcategories, whether representing income or expenses, are labeled *Sub*.

Actually, your Quicken accounts constitute another "category" type. At the end of the category list, note that Quicken has added a line for each of the accounts in your file. In this context, accounts are referred to as *transfer* categories. The entry in the Type column for the accounts is the type of account (bank, credit card, and so on). In Chapter 8, you'll see how assigning an account name as a category allows you to record money that you move among your accounts.

NOTE

If you want to limit the list to categories of a particular type, click the appropriate tab at the top of the window.

In the column labeled *Tax*, an entry of **Tax** indicates that the category on that line is somehow tax-related. Again, this doesn't mean the category has been set up to help you with income tax preparation (see the next section for instructions on setting up to use Quicken to help do your taxes).

137

The final column, labeled *Description*, displays the full description of the category.

Functions you can perform with the category list include:

- Adding categories from the built-in categories that come with Quicken
- Creating new categories from scratch
- Modifying existing categories
- Removing categories from the list
- Managing supercategories

Adding Categories from the Built-in Collection

Quicken's built-in categories are always available to add to your category list individually or *en masse*. This can be handy if you run a small business and need only a few business-related categories. Instead of clogging your category list with the entire built-in set, you can add just the categories you need. This technique is also the easiest way to add back a built-in category you previously deleted.

To add built-in categories, click the **Add** button at the top of the Category List window. The box shown in Figure 7.3 appears.

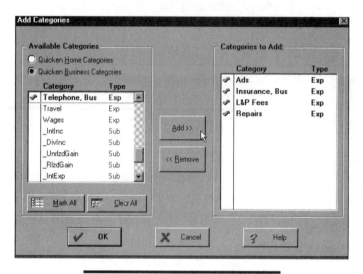

Figure 7.3 The Add Categories box.

At the top left, select the set of built-in categories you want to choose from: **Home** or **Business**. The list at the bottom left changes accordingly. For each category you want to add, scroll through the list to find it, then click it to mark it with a check. When you've checked off all the desired categories, click **Add** to copy them to the Categories to Add list on the right side. Then click **OK** to add the chosen categories to your Category List.

Creating New Categories from Scratch

To add a category of your own to the list, click the **New** button and fill out the Set Up Category box, described in the previous section.

Modifying Existing Categories

To change the definition of a category, highlight the category in the list, then click the **Edit** button. Aside from the title, the box that appears is exactly like the Set Up Category box and works the same way.

Removing Existing Categories

It's a good idea to remove categories you don't use from the category list—the fewer there are, the easier it is to scroll to and spot the category you want, and the faster QuickFill will come up with a match. To remove a category, highlight it in the list, then click **Delete**. Quicken presents you with a small box asking if you really want to remove the category. To proceed, click **OK**.

Managing Supercategories

Supercategories are new in Quicken 5. They allow you to summarize groups of related categories so that you can see broad trends in income and spending. Quicken's built-in categories are already assigned to four supercategories: Income supercategories for salary, "other" income, and expense supercategories for discretionary and nondiscretionary spending.

As you'd expect, Quicken lets you modify the supercategories as you wish. You can assign any given category to any of the available supercategories. You can create, rename, or delete supercategories at will.

To work with supercategories, click the **Super** button on the Category List window. The window shown in Figure 7.4 appears.

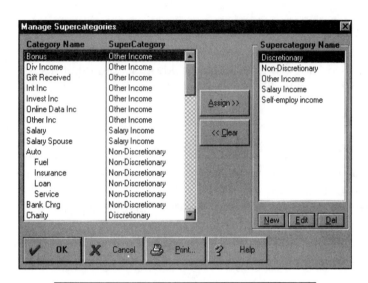

Figure 7.4 The Manage Supercategories window.

The list in the left half of the window shows you the current super-category assignment for each category. The one on the right displays the supercategories themselves and lets you edit them.

To assign a category to a supercategory or to change the current assignment:

1. Highlight the category you want to work with in the list on the left.

2. Highlight the supercategory you want to assign it to in the list on the right.

3. Click **Assign**.

You can also remove the current supercategory assignment altogether. Highlight the category name and click **Clear**.

To add a new supercategory, click the **New** button at the bottom of the list on the right, type in the name you've chosen, and click **OK**. To change a supercategory name, highlight the supercategory and click **Edit**. To delete a supercategory—well, you know what to do.

Creating and Using Classes

As you learned in Chapter 3, Quicken's classes are designed for customized classification schemes. For this reason, Quicken doesn't come with any built-in class definitions—you have to create any classes you want from scratch. You can do this while you're working, in the process of assigning a transaction to the class you want to create. Alternatively, you can create classes in advance. Both techniques are covered below.

Assigning Classes to Transactions and Setting Up New Classes

To assign a class to a register transaction, online payment, or check, enter the class in the Category field. Probably the quickest way to do this requires some typing. Here's how:

1. After entering the transaction's category, and the subcategory, if any, type / (the slash character, on the same key as the question mark).

2. Begin typing the class name. Just as with categories, QuickFill will complete the entry for you if any classes match the characters you type. If you're entering a new class, QuickFill won't help—just type in the entire name.

Here's an example of a completed Category field with a class entry:

3/25/96	316	Atlantic Energy Systems	75	45
		Utilities/2nd home Winter vacation		

If the class you've entered doesn't yet exist, Quicken detects this when you move out of the Category field. You'll see a simple Set Up Class box shown in Figure 7.5.

Here, Quicken has already entered the name of the class from your entry in the Category field. Type in a longer description if you like in the provided field. (The Copy Number field is for income tax preparation; see "Using Classes for Income Tax Preparation" later in this chapter.) Click OK when you've completed the box.

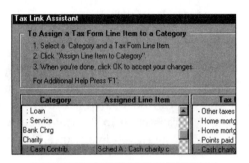

Figure 7.5 The Set Up Class box.

142

NOTE

Using the mouse, here's how to assign a class to the transaction you're entering: Switch to the Class List, a large window containing all the classes you've set up, by opening the Lists menu and choosing **Class**. In the Class list, double-click on the class you want to assign. Quicken automatically returns to the transaction you were working on, entering the chosen class in the Category field for you.

Managing Classes with the Class List

You can add, edit, and delete classes using the class list. To display the list, open the Lists menu and choose **Class**. You'll see a simple list showing any classes you've created with their descriptions. Click the buttons at the upper left to modify the list:

Add—Click here to display the Set Up Class box (Figure 7.5). Type in a name and description for the class. If you're using classes for tax accounting as described below, enter the tax form copy number in the corresponding field.

Edit—To change the name, description, or copy number assignment for an existing class, highlight the class in the Class List window, then click **Edit**. Except for the title, the Edit Class box is exactly the same as the Set Up Class box used to create new classes.

Delete—To remove a class from the list, highlight it and click **Delete**.

Setting up Categories and Classes for Income Tax Preparation

For many people, the ability to automate income tax preparation is one of the real joys of using Quicken. If you couple Quicken with tax preparation software, you can basically press a button and sit back while your tax forms print out.

NOTE

All popular tax preparation programs work well with Quicken. TurboTax, the top-selling product of this type, is now published by Intuit and is especially well integrated with Quicken.

143

But even without special tax software Quicken can total up all the numbers you'll need to fill out the 1040 form. To prepare your income taxes, you just transfer Quicken's totals to the appropriate lines on the forms.

However, you can only take advantage of Quicken for tax preparation if you set up your records correctly ahead of time. Again, setting up a category as "tax-related" is of no value in preparing your tax forms. The key step is this: *You must assign each tax-related category to the proper line of the proper tax form.* Before you do that, though, you have to make sure that you've enabled this Quicken feature.

Activating Tax Form Assignments

When you're setting up a new category (or editing an existing one) with the Set Up Category box, you should see a space labeled *Form* in the Tax area. If so, you're ready for tax accounting with Quicken. If the Form area isn't showing, however, you have an extra step ahead of you. Go on and complete the category you're working on, but at the first opportunity you should turn on the feature that lets you assign tax form information to your categories. Here's how:

1. From the Category List window, click the **Options** button. The Options box appears.

2. Click the **General** button. In the General Options box, check the box labeled **Use Tax Schedules with Categories**. Click **OK** to return to the Options box, then **Close** to return to Quicken itself.

Assigning Tax Form Line Information to Categories

The crucial step in setting up for accurate tax accounting with Quicken is to link each relevant category to the proper line on the tax form. Of course, you only need to worry about categories covering items that you must report on your tax forms as income or deductible expenses—ignore categories for food or personal entertainment that aren't deductible.

Quicken gives you two ways to link a category to the right tax form line. You can:

• Select the proper line from the list in the Form area of the Set Up Category box; or

• From the Category List window, click the **Tax Link** button. The window that appears (Figure 7.6) lets you set or change the tax form assignments for all your categories, and you get helpful information about each tax form line item to boot. To link a category, highlight it in the list on the left side of the window, highlight the correct tax form line in the list on the right, and click **Assign Line Item to Category**.

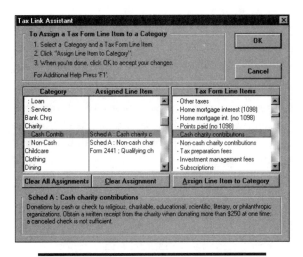

Figure 7.6 The Tax Link Assistant window.

Using Subcategories for Tax Accounting

If a single category can include both tax- and nontax-related items, or items that should be recorded on separate lines of your tax forms, you should divide the category. One way to do this is to create subcategories that distinguish between the items, assigning one subcategory to a tax form line while leaving the other subcategory unassigned.

For example, childcare expenses can be deducted only when the care is provided while the parent works. If you send your kids to daycare on shopping days as well as work days, you should set up two subcategories for the Childcare category, assigning the one for work-related daycare to tax form 2441. If the payments you make to the daycare center cover both types of service, you can split these transactions and assign each portion of the split to the appropriate subcategory. When you prepare a Tax Schedule report only the tax-deductible daycare expenses will show up, allowing you to transfer the totals directly to your form 2441. You can still see how much you're spending in total on childcare with reports that aren't restricted to categories assigned to tax forms. (See Chapter 10 to learn about Quicken reports.)

Using Classes for Income Tax Preparation

There are two ways you can use classes for tax accounting purposes. The first is as an alternative to subcategories to subdivide categories that cover both tax and nontax-related items (see the section just previous).

Using classes is easier if you have many categories in which both types of transactions occur. This might be the case if you use your personal checking account to run a part-time small business. You probably have business and personal phone bills, business and personal entertainment expenses, and so on. Instead of creating subcategories in each of these categories, the simpler approach is to create classes called "Business" and "Personal" and assign one of them to each payment and deposit in your account. When it's time to prepare your tax returns you can customize a Tax Schedule report, restricting it to transactions assigned to the Business class.

The second tax-oriented use for classes lets you differentiate between items in the same category that should be reported on different copies of a particular tax form. This is most often useful if you have file two or more copies of Schedule C (Profit or Loss from Business) covering separate business activities. To distinguish between the bills and income that apply to your mail-order haberdashery and those for your roadside organic produce stand, you would create two different classes, "Haberdashery" and "Produce." When you set up the classes, assign them in the Copy Number field (see Figure 7.5) to copy 1 and copy 2, respectively. If you enter the appropriate class for every transaction, Quicken will be able to extract separate totals for each business in tax reports and when you use your records with tax preparation software.

Summary

You should now have a good grasp of the steps required to tailor your lists of categories and classes to match your individual circumstances. In the chapters to follow, you'll bring all your knowledge of Quicken to bear on the true goals of accurate financial recordkeeping: safeguarding and building your net worth.

CHAPTER EIGHT:

Real-World Financial Management with Quicken:

Tracking Savings, Credit Cards, Cash, and Loans

These days, most of us lead complicated financial lives. Even for people squarely in the middle class, the simple days when a single checking account and perhaps a separate savings account would suffice are long gone.

In the typical case, there's the main bank account used to pay bills, money market fund and CD accounts for medium-term cash storage, and your credit card accounts (who has just one credit card?). You may have an IRA or 401(K) plan, you probably own some mutual funds, and you may even hold some individual stocks or bonds. If you own your home your equity in it makes a substantial contribution to your net worth. And there's that monthly mortgage payment to contend with, consuming a third or more of your income and heavily influencing your tax situation.

If you want to bring Quicken's full financial-analysis power to bear, you're going to need a separate Quicken account to keep track of each of these components of your overall financial picture. You're already aware that Quicken lets you set up as many as 255 different accounts in each Quicken file. In this chapter, you'll learn all about using and managing a complete set of accounts in Quicken.

After an overview of the types of Quicken accounts, we'll review the steps required to set up new accounts. You'll then learn to account for money that flows between one part of your financial universe and another with Quicken "transfer" transactions. And you'll see how to keep track of specific assets and liabilities, including your savings accounts, credit cards, cash, and major assets and loans such as your home and its mortgage. We'll leave investments to Chapter 9.

About Quicken Accounts

Quicken offers a total of six different types of accounts, each tailored to a specific purpose:

- *Bank accounts* record transactions in your real-life checking, savings, and money market accounts.

- *Credit card accounts* track all your credit card purchases, charges, and payments.

- *Cash accounts* monitor cash transactions.

- *Asset accounts* are used to manage property, business equipment, or accounts receivable (the amounts owed to you by your customers).

- *Liability accounts* are used to follow your mortgages, loans, and accounts payable (the amounts your business owes for goods and services you've purchased but not yet paid for).

- *Investment accounts* keep track of investments such as stocks, bonds, mutual funds, and so on.

All six account types have many features in common, but each works slightly differently. We'll cover the details here and in Chapter 9.

Managing Quicken Accounts

To list the accounts you have, change or delete them, or create new ones, use the Account List window (Figure 8.1). Display the window by clicking on the **Accounts** button on the Iconbar:

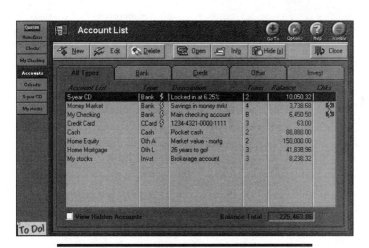

Figure 8.1 The Account List window showing a variety of Quicken accounts.

The tabs at the top of the account list let you choose which accounts appear in the list: you can see them all, or select by account type (if you click the **Other** tab, the list displays cash, asset, and liability accounts). The buttons in the account list button bar work as follows:

- The **New**, **Edit**, and **Delete** buttons let you create, modify, or remove accounts in the list.

- To display the register of any listed account, you can highlight it in the list and click **Open**—but it's easier simply to double-click on the account.

- Click the **Info** button to see or change additional information about the account (see Figure 8.2 for an example).

149

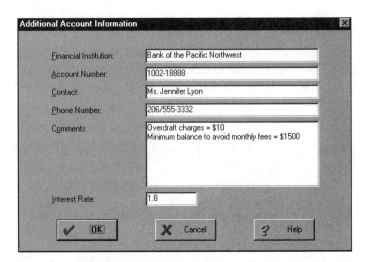

Figure 8.2 This window lists additional information about the account.

- To make an account "invisible," highlight it in the list and click **Hide**. This can be helpful if the account contains historical records that don't bear on your current situation, but must be preserved for your files. You can also hide accounts on a trial basis, to see how your financial situation would change without their contribution.

Setting up New Accounts

You learned how to set up new accounts back in Chapter 2. But let's review the procedure here:

1. Begin by opening the account list.

2. Click the **New** button to begin creating the account. A Create New Account window appears with buttons for the various types of Quicken accounts (Figure 8.3).

3. Click the button for the type of account you're creating. You can use a Savings account if you're tracking a CD. Use an Investment account to manage mutual funds as well as stocks, bonds, and commodities.

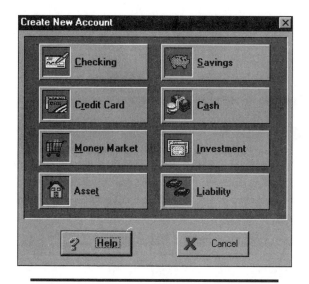

Figure 8.3 The Create New Account window.

NOTE

Note that the Create New Account window contains buttons for eight types of accounts. Quicken only has six account types, so why the extra buttons? Here's your answer: The **Checking**, **Savings**, and **Money Market** buttons all create functionally identical Quicken "bank" accounts. The only difference between the buttons is the name Quicken suggests for the account: "Checking" if you click the **Checking** button, "Savings" if you click **Savings**, and so on.

4. Quicken displays a sequence of EasyStep panels prompting you for the information required to start the account. Complete each panel in turn, clicking the **Next** button at the bottom right to advance to the next panel.

5. When you've finished supplying information, Quicken displays your entries in one or more Summary panels. Click **Done** when you reach the final panel to confirm the information and create the account.

151

Once you've created the account, it appears in the account list. Open its register by double-clicking on the account in the list.

Tracking Savings Accounts, Money Market Funds, and CDs

If you maintain a passbook savings account or have a money market account or CD (*certificate of deposit*) at your bank, a savings and loan association, or a money market fund, you should use a Quicken "bank" account to track the money you keep there.

To get the most from online banking, you should keep your savings or money market funds at the same institution where you have your main online checking account. That way, you can set up the savings account for online banking too, and then use online banking to transfer money back and forth between the two accounts as your needs dictate.

Create the new account with the steps outlined earlier. In the Create New Account window, click **Savings** or **Money Market** (it doesn't matter which, since they both create Quicken bank accounts, identical except for the account name). Enter the balance from your last statement as the opening balance of the new account.

If you have arranged with the financial institution to use online banking with the account, activate this feature as you create the account by clicking the appropriate button during the account setup process. Many money market accounts come with check-writing privileges, in which case you can use the account with online bill payment if you like. If you do activate online services, be ready to supply the additional information Quicken will request.

Once the account has been created, record transactions in the new account's register just as you would in your checking account. When you make a deposit, the amount of the transaction goes in the Deposit column; when you make a withdrawal, enter the amount in the Payment column.

Transferring Funds between Quicken Accounts

You learned back in Chapter 4 how to use online banking to transfer funds between two accounts at the same financial institution. Here, you'll learn a complementary skill, and one with broader application: how to use Quicken *transfers* to account for the movement of funds between any two parts of your financial universe.

When funds move from one location to another, Quicken needs two transactions to accurately reflect the event: a withdrawal or payment transaction in one account and a deposit transaction in the other. But your work is easy—you just enter the details of the transfer once, and Quicken automatically creates the mirrored transactions in the two accounts. In some cases, in fact, Quicken handles the whole process for you based on the activity in your accounts.

To record these paired transfer transactions Quicken uses the Category field in a special way. In each transaction of the pair, Quicken simply lists the name of the *other* account as the Category field entry. The account name is listed in brackets, like this: [My Checking], to distinguish it from a standard category.

Online Funds Transfers

Let's start with an obvious example. Say you bank online and you want to shore up a sagging checking account balance with funds from your savings account. In this case, once you complete the online funds transfer, Quicken will automatically record the necessary transfer transactions in the registers of the two accounts.

The procedure goes like this: Open the Online Banking window and select the institution where you have both accounts. When you click the **Transfer Funds** button, Quicken asks you to select the account that you're moving the money *from* and the one where the funds are *headed*. When you then click **Transmit**, Quicken sends in the transfer instructions. As soon as this is complete, Quicken records a transfer transaction in each account. As Figure 8.4 shows, the register entry for each transaction lists the other account in the Category field.

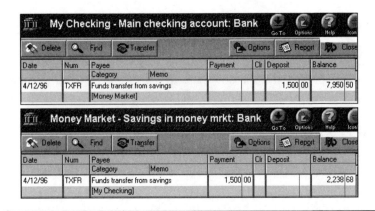

Figure 8.4 A pair of transactions entered by Quicken in two separate accounts to record an online funds transfer. Note the entries in the Category field.

Entering Other Types of Transfers

But what if you move funds between accounts at two separate institutions? Suppose you have your checking account at one bank and your savings account at the bank across the street. In an old-fashioned, nononline transaction, you write a $500 check payable to CASH at the first bank. When the teller hands you the money, you walk it over to the second bank to make your monthly contribution to your savings. How would you account for this transaction in Quicken?

You can start from either Quicken account, but it's a little easier if you begin from the account where the money came *from*. In this case, that's your checking account. Switching to the checking account register, enter the transfer as follows:

1. Click the **Transfer** button in the register's button bar:

2. Fill in the transaction details (date, description, and amount) in the Transfer Money Between Accounts box, shown in Figure

8.5. The entry you make in the Description field here will appear in the Payee field in the register in bank accounts.

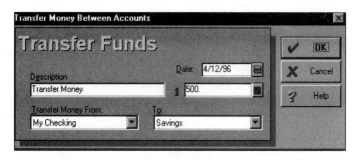

Figure 8.5 The Transfer Money Between Accounts box.

3. Use the two fields at the bottom of the box to specify which account the money came from and which it went to. Because you started with the checking account, it should already be listed in the Transfer Money From field.

4. Click **OK** to finalize the transfer information. Quicken creates the matching pair of transfer transactions, inserting them into the accounts you specified. You're returned to the register where you can inspect the transaction and add any missing details, such as the check number or a memo.

Entering Transfer Transactions Directly in the Register

If you've used earlier versions of Quicken, you know that you can also enter transfer transactions directly into the register. Once you know your way around in Quicken, this technique is probably a little faster.

Starting from either account involved in the transfer, enter a new transaction. When you get to the category field, just use QuickFill to help you enter the name of the other account: begin typing the account name until QuickFill completes it for you (QuickFill adds the brackets signifying a transfer, too). As an alternative to QuickFill, you can scroll to the bottom of the pop-up category list—that's where the account names are listed—and click on the correct account:

NOTE

The Transfer Money choice at the very top of the pop-up category list is just another way to open the Transfer Money Between Accounts box, described earlier.

When you record the new transaction, Quicken automatically creates its match in the other account.

Switching between Paired Transfer Transactions

You can switch directly from a transfer transaction in one account to the paired transaction in another. With the transfer transaction highlighted in the register, press **Ctrl-X**. Quicken switches instantly to the parallel transaction in the other account.

Tracking Transferred Funds in Split Transactions

Quicken can handle more complicated funds transfers that take place as part of a larger transaction. Suppose that when you deposit your monthly paycheck at the bank, you place a portion of the funds into your savings account while the bulk of the money goes to your checking account. You can use a Quicken split transaction to record this event, transferring only the money that wound up in your savings account.

Starting from your checking account, you would begin entering a new deposit transaction, entering the total amount of your paycheck in the Deposit field. Then split the transaction (click the **Splits** button). In the top line of the Splits window, enter a category for the paycheck (like **Salary**) and leave the amount set to the total you deposited.

In the second line, create the transfer: Use QuickFill or the drop-down category list to place the name of the savings account to which you transferred the funds. In the amount column for this line, type the transferred amount as a *negative* number. Figure 8.6 shows how the completed Splits window might look.

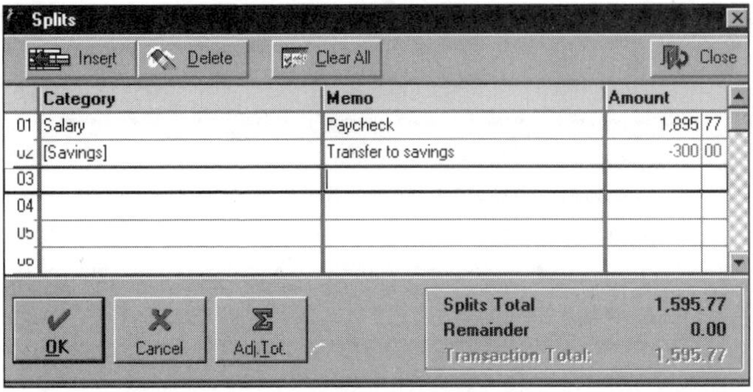

Figure 8.6 The Splits window as it might look when you place funds into two accounts with one deposit.

When you click **OK** to return to the register, Quicken recalculates the amount of the transaction so that your checking account balance correctly reflects only the funds you placed in it. If you switch to the savings account register, you'll see a parallel transfer deposit showing only the amount you transferred in.

Tracking Credit Cards

Although you can record credit card payments you make in your regular checking account and leave it at that, a separate Quicken credit card account lets you monitor your credit card usage much more closely. And if you sign up for a credit card with online accounting, Quicken will automatically record all your credit card transactions.

A separate Quicken credit card account offers the kind of close-up detail that's needed in a sensible financial management program. While it won't enforce discipline on your spending, a credit card account will make it easier to spot your purchase patterns. If a crunch comes, it can tell you your current balance and, more importantly, how much of your credit limit is left. In addition, when your payment is due, Quicken will automatically create the online payment (or print a check). And Quicken makes it easy to check your records against your monthly credit card statement, reconciling your account as you would a Quicken checking account.

NOTE

Use a credit card account to keep track of a line of credit such as the kind based on the equity in your home. After all, a line of credit functions very much like a credit card—you use it to make purchases whenever you decide to, and the amount you owe changes all the time.

158 Setting up a Credit Card Account

If you plan to use Quicken's online credit card accounting features, you must sign up for online credit card services with a participating financial institution. Intuit, Quicken's publisher, offers the "Quicken credit card" (it's actually sponsored by The Travelers'). You can access an American Express account through Quicken as well. And many of the banks participating in Quicken's online banking program will be offering their own online-ready credit cards.

To create a credit card account, display the Account List window, click the **New** button, and then click **Credit Card**. In the window that appears (Figure 8.7), step through the panels in succession, supply the requested information as you go:

1. Type in the name you want for the account and if you like, enter a more detailed description.

2. In a credit card account, the balance represents how much you owe; enter this amount from your last statement in the *Balance Due* field along with the statement date.

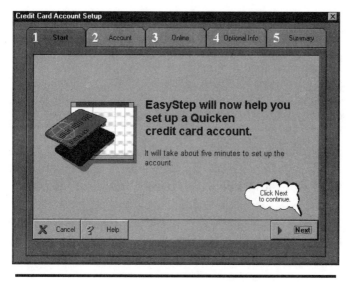

Figure 8.7 Set up a new credit card account in this window.

3. In the Online panel, click the **Yes** button if your credit card is activated for online use. Quicken will then present several panels asking for pertinent information. First, choose the name of the sponsoring institution or **Quicken Credit Card** from the drop-down list. If you've selected a Quicken credit card, all you need to add is the credit card number and indicate whether you receive your statement on diskette or (preferably) via modem. For credit cards from other institutions, enter the account number, indicate whether this account is for a credit card or a line of credit, and type in your social security number and the bank's routing number.

4. Type in the credit limit for the card.

5. If you like, enter miscellaneous information about the card on the *Optional Information* panel, including the institution that issued the card, the account number, the institution's phone number, the current interest rate, and any additional notes you want to keep. Note that this information is particularly valuable for credit card accounts that aren't set up for online use.

6. Review the information in the Summary panels, clicking **Done** when you're satisfied with the entries. The new credit card account appears in your account list. Double-click on the account to open its register.

Entering Credit Card Transactions

As shown in Figure 8.8, the register of a credit card account looks and works much as the register for your checking account. As you'd expect, a few details vary.

At the bottom right, the amount of your remaining credit appears just above the balance owing. The amount columns are labeled *Charge* and *Payment* instead of Payment and Deposit. Transactions that you have to pay for, such as purchases, finance charges, or fees, have their amounts listed in the Charge field. Transactions that reduce what you owe on your account—these include payments you make as well as credits for returned merchandise and the like—have their amounts listed in the Payment field.

160

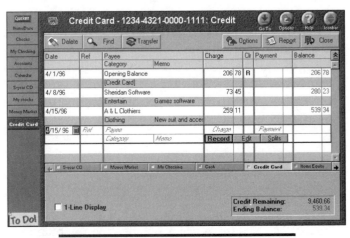

Figure 8.8 The credit card account register.

The beauty of an online credit card account is that you never need enter another credit card transaction by hand. Instead, Quicken adds them to your account for you from your online statement. In fact, you should actively avoid entering transactions manually—if you make a mistake, you may wind up with duplicate entries in your account and an incorrect balance. To check the bank's work, you can still compare the entries made from your online statement against your paper receipts.

If you don't have an online account, you type transactions into your credit card account yourself using the same methods you would to record them in your checking account.

Obtaining an Online Credit Card Statement

Before you can receive an online statement for your Quicken credit card account, you must take care of the same preliminaries for any online work with Quicken: You must set up your modem in Quicken and then obtain an Intuit membership. See Chapter 2 for instructions. Of course, you also need a real-life credit card account that's set up for online use.

With these first steps complete, here's how to obtain an online credit card statement:

1. Click the **Online** button on the Iconbar to open the Online Banking window.

2. In the financial institution field at the top left, select the name of the institution that issued the credit card, or choose **Quicken Credit Card**.

3. Click **Get Online Data**. Quicken goes on line to get the latest available statement from the chosen institution. (If you have other accounts at the institution, you'll receive information about them as well). The Transmission Summary window will remind you as the due date on your credit card bill approaches.

4. Review the statement summary in the Online Banking window. Quicken lists the balance for the credit card account in red if you owe money, and in black if you have an unused credit on the

account. Highlight the credit card account and click the **Payment Info** button to display the payment due date and the minimum payment amount from your most recent monthly statement.

5. To have Quicken add the new credit card transactions to your account, highlight the account in the upper portion of the window, then click **Update Register**. In the Update Register window, notice that each new transaction listed has been assigned a category based on the merchant number. Proceed as outlined in Chapter 4 to review the transactions, changing payee detail and category assignments as necessary.

6. Click **Add to Register** to insert the new transactions into your credit card register.

Reconciling Your Credit Card Account

When you receive your paper credit card statement from the bank, use it to reconcile your credit card account in Quicken. The process parallels the one you learned for reconciling checking accounts in Chapter 4. Gather the statement (and your paper receipts too, if you're using an online account) and get to work:

1. Switch to the credit card account you want to reconcile, then click the **Reconcile** button on the Iconbar. The Reconcile Account window appears (Figure 8.9).

2. Here, if you have an online credit account, choose whether to reconcile to your paper statement or the online statement. If you're reconciling to your paper statement (or if you don't have an online account), copy the date and amounts from the statement into the appropriate fields.

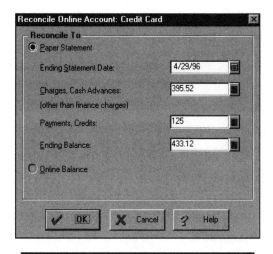

Figure 8.9 The Reconcile Account window.

NOTE

If you're reconciling a nononline account, Quicken asks you to copy the month's finance charges into the Reconcile Account window, and will automatically add a corresponding transaction to the account. You don't need to enter this amount if you have an online account since it will be added to your account when you update it via your online statement.

3. Click **OK** to proceed to the main reconciliation window. Just as when reconciling a checking account, mark as cleared the transactions listed here if they appear on your credit card statement so that a yellow check mark appears in the Clr column. To enter any transactions that appear on your statement but not in your account, click the **New** button to move to the register; close the register when you've finished with it.

4. When the amount at Difference equals zero, you've successfully reconciled the account. Click **Finished** to return to the register. (If you have problems with reconciling, read the pointers on reconciling bank accounts in Chapter 4).

Paying Your Credit Card Bill

The method you'll use to pay your credit card bill depends on whether the card is set up for online recordkeeping or not.

Paying an Online Credit Card Bill

The simplest method to make payments on an online credit card is to use online banking to transfer funds from another account at the same institution into the credit card account. This only works if both the credit card and the account for the payment are at the same institution, and if the institution allows transfers between credit card accounts and other accounts. Follow the steps detailed in Chapter 4 for making such transfers.

TIP

If your bank permits transfers between your online credit card and checking accounts, you can make them in both directions. To give yourself a cash advance, transfer funds from the credit card account to the checking account.

If you can't handle an online credit card bill with a funds transfer, you can still cover it with an online payment. Here's how to proceed:

1. Go online to get your current balance as described in "Obtaining an Online Credit Card Statement," earlier in this chapter.

2. After Quicken receives the current statement, highlight the credit card account in the Online Banking window and click the **Payment Info** button.

3. In the Payment Information window, click the **Make Payment** button. You'll see a window like the one shown in Figure 8.10.

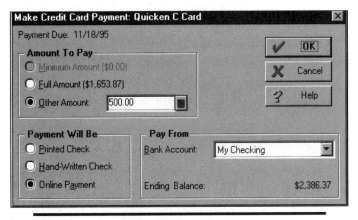

Figure 8.10 Use this window to make payments on an online credit card account.

4. Here, indicate the amount you want to pay, the type of payment you'll be making (online payment, printed Quicken check, or handwritten check) and the account from which the funds will come. Click **OK** to make the payment.

5. If you've selected an online payment or printed check, Quicken displays the Write Checks window with the check already completed based on your entries. Review the check details, then record it. You'll still have to send in the online payment or print and send the check, of course. If you chose a handwritten payment, Quicken enters a corresponding transaction in the register. Again, you'll then need to write out and send a matching check.

Paying a Regular Credit Card Bill

If your credit card is not set up for online use, the simplest way to pay the bill is at the time you reconcile the account. After you complete the reconciliation as outlined above, Quicken offers to help you make the payment, as shown in Figure 8.11.

Figure 8.11 The Make Credit Card Payment box.

Select the account from which you want to make the payment and the type of payment you want to make: a printed Quicken check, a hand-written check, or an online payment. When you click **OK**, you'll be taken either to the Write Checks window where you can complete the information for check or online payment, or to the register, where you can finish a transaction for your handwritten check. After you record any of these transactions, remember to actually make the payment: Go online to deliver the online payment, print and mail the Quicken check, or write and mail your own handwritten one.

Tracking Cash in Quicken

Unless your cash transactions are large or numerous, the easiest way to account for them is to record them in your regular bank accounts. Should your needs dictate otherwise, however, Quicken provides a separate account type just for tracking cash transactions.

Recording Cash Transactions in Your Checking and Savings Accounts

When you withdraw cash from your checking or savings account, you can record the withdrawal as a payment transaction in the account. If you want to keep track of where you spent the money, just enter a description of the purchase in the Memo field and assign the transaction to the appropriate category. If you spent the cash on more than one type of item, you can split the transaction to record separate categories for each item—see Chapter 3 for instructions on splitting transactions. Don't worry about accounting for every last penny of a cash withdrawal—you can always categorize the amount that's left over as *Misc* (miscellaneous).

Similarly, if you have cash income, just record it as a deposit in your register. If you spend the cash you earn before depositing it, you need a special technique. In this case, you should still start by entering a deposit transaction. Before you record it, however, you'll split the deposit to list your spending (Figure 8.12).

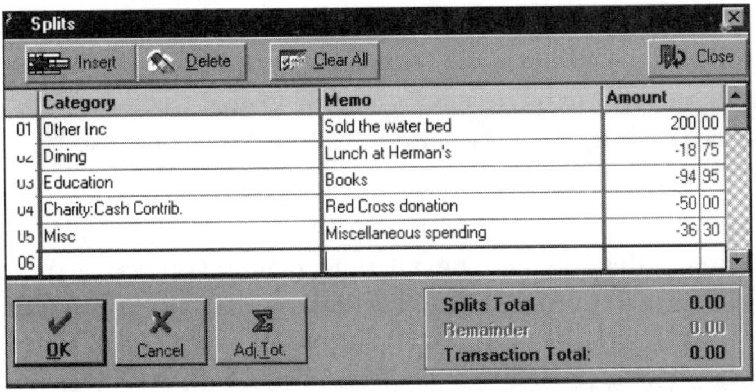

167

Figure 8.12 Recording cash income and spending in the checking account register as a split transaction.

In the Splits window, type the entire amount of your cash income on the first line as a positive amount; you can enter **Other inc** as the category or create a new category for cash income. On the remaining lines, list each item you bought, assigning each an appropriate expense category and entering the purchase amount *as a negative number*. When you close the Splits window, Quicken will add up all the numbers—they should equal zero if you accounted for all the money spent—and place this amount in the Deposit column. Now you've recorded the income and your spending, but your checking account balance hasn't changed—which reflects the fact you never really made a deposit.

Using a Separate Cash Account

If you want detailed records of all your cash purchases and income, you can set up a separate account devoted strictly to cash transactions. A Quicken cash account works almost exactly like checking and savings accounts, so you should feel right at home.

Of course, a Quicken cash account doesn't represent an actual bank account (unless perhaps your spouse serves as your personal banker!). Instead, it simply represents the sum total of all the cash you can lay claim to, whether it's under the mattress or under the seat of your car.

Quicken doesn't force you to record every $3 magazine or book of stamps you buy in your cash account. Instead, you can enter the important cash transactions, and have Quicken adjust the balance to cover miscellaneous amounts.

The basic procedure for setting up a cash account is outlined at the beginning of this chapter. The only information you need to supply is the account name and the balance (how much cash you have) as of today's date.

After creating the account, switch to its register by double-clicking the account in the account list. The register of a cash account looks almost identical to the one in your checking account, though some of the columns have different names. Instead of a Num field, there's one

168

labeled *Ref*; instead of Payment and Deposit, there are *Spend* and *Receive*.

Transferring Cash to and from Your Checking Account

Most often, the cash you have comes from a bank withdrawal (either at a teller's window or from an ATM machine. To account for the movement of money from your bank to your pocket, set up a transfer in Quicken. As you learned in the section on savings accounts, a transfer is a pair of transactions in the two Quicken accounts involved in an exchange of funds.

To set up a transfer for a cash withdrawal, switch to the register of the checking or savings account where the withdrawal was made. After clicking the **Transfer** button, fill out the Transfer Money Between Accounts window (refer back to Figure 8.5), selecting the cash account as the destination for the transfer.

When you've completed the box, Quicken creates the pair of transfer transactions, adding one to each account. The transaction in the checking account lists the cash account as its category; in the cash account transactions, the Category field displays the name of the checking account. If you're recording an ATM withdrawal, you should change the entry in the Num field to **ATM** for the transaction in your checking account.

Adjusting the Balance of a Cash Account

Periodically, you should adjust the balance in your cash account to reflect the cash you actually have on hand. Quicken handles the adjustment for you, automatically creating a single transaction that brings the account balance into line. To make the adjustment, begin from the register of your cash account, open the Activities menu, and choose **Update Balance —> Update Cash Balance**. Quicken displays the Update Account Balance box (Figure 8.13).

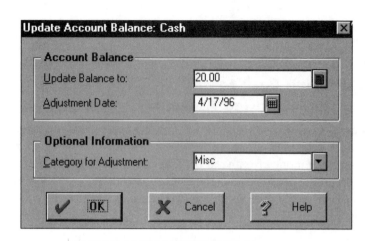

Figure 8.13 Update Account Balance box.

170

All you have to do is total up your cash on hand and type this amount in the window. If you like, you can assign the transaction to a category such as *Misc* (for miscellaneous). When you click **OK** to close the window, Quicken calculates the amount of the needed balance-correcting transaction, adding it to your cash account. The amount listed at Ending Balance in the lower right of the register should now equal your cash on hand.

Monitoring Loans and Assets

Your net worth probably includes of variety of important assets and liabilities that don't show up in your checking, savings, and credit card accounts. Of course, if you own your home, the equity may well be the largest single asset you have. Likewise, your outstanding mortgage balance probably dwarfs the amount you owe on your credit cards. In addition, though, you may also be paying off significant loans on a car or your college education.

Quicken makes it easy to keep track of all types of assets and liabilities in special asset and liability accounts. Fundamentally, these are no different than the other Quicken accounts you're accustomed to, but they do have a few special features for the tasks they're designed for. Assets you might want to monitor with a Quicken asset account include your IRA, the value of your home and the improvements you make to it, investment real estate, and collections of fine art or antiques. On the liability side, you can set up accounts for your mortgage and each major loan.

Whether or not you make use of these additional account types is a matter of personal taste and judgment. Since most mortgages and other major loans have fixed payment schedules, you may be content to make your monthly payments knowing that the loan will eventually be paid off. In that case, you can record the payments in your regular checking account and leave it at that.

For most people, though, that won't be enough—especially when Quicken can automatically *amortize* your loan for you, showing just how much you're spending on both principal and interest each month. That's perfect for tracking tax-deductible interest payments, and it's a good way to watch your equity grow. But to take advantage of this feature, you'll have to set up a separate liability account for each amortized loan. And in any case, Quicken can calculate your net worth accurately only if you set up accounts for all your major assets and liabilities.

Tracking Assets

If you're a homeowner, your home is almost certainly your most important asset. It makes sense to track its value over time in a Quicken asset account. In tandem with a liability account for your mortgage, this will let you monitor the growth of your equity over the years. But it's also an important tool for tax purposes. You can also use assets accounts to monitor the value of other assets that aren't particularly liquid, such as artwork, antiques, or collections of coins or stamps. Finally, asset accounts are good for keeping track of loans you make to others (in this case, you'll use steps similar to the ones for setting up a mortgage or other loan on which you owe the money—see "Tracking Loans," later in this chapter).

Create an asset account just like you would any other Quicken account, choosing **Asset** in the Create New Account window. As you move through the panels Quicken displays, enter the account name, the value of the asset on the opening date, and tax-related information if desired.

When you open the asset account register (Figure 8.14), note that the amount columns (corresponding to Payment and Deposit in the checking account) are labeled *Decrease* and *Increase*. Enter transactions that increase the value of your asset by placing the amount in the Increase field.

Date	Ref	Payee		Decrease	Clr	Increase	Balance	
		Category	Memo					
8/15/91		Opening Balance			R	189,000 00	189,000 00	
		[Home Equity]						
7/31/92		Room addition/remodel			R	25,000 00	214,000 00	
		[2nd mortgage]						
1/ 1/93		Market value adjustment		15,000 00	R		199,000 00	
10/ 1/93		New deck			R	4,000 00	203,000 00	
		[My Checking]						
1/ 1/94		Market value adjustment			R	5,000 00	208,000 00	

Home Equity - Market value - mortg: Asset — Go To, Options, Help, Iconbar — Delete, Find, Transfer, Options, Report, Close — Record, Edit, Splits

Figure 8.14 An Asset account, used here to track the value of a home.

For a mortgage, you should record Increase transactions for anything that adds "permanently" to the value of your home. Permanent home improvements increase the tax basis of your home, decreasing the taxable profit you'll realize when you sell the home (consult a tax professional for details).

To adjust the account value to reflect changes in the real estate market, enter a transaction in the appropriate amount listing the payee as "market value adjustment" or the like (when you sell the home, you'll still be able to calculate the tax basis by preparing a report filtered to display only the other transactions). The simplest way to alter the account value is by opening the Activities menu and choosing **Update**

172

Balances —> **Update Cash Balance**. Type in the current value of the account (in this case the current market value of the home). When you click **OK**, Quicken calculates the adjustment needed to reach the new balance and adds a transaction in that amount.

Tracking Your Mortgage and Other Loans

In Quicken, you keep track of your mortgage or other major loans in liability accounts. But instead of creating the liability account yourself, let Quicken do it in the process of setting up the loan details. As you set up the loan, Quicken coaches you through the process of setting up a payment method, online or otherwise—after you've finished the setup. You never have to enter the payment details again.

Before you start setting up the loan, there may be one key step to attend to. If you plan to pay the bill with an online repeating payment, the kind the bank makes for you every month automatically, you must set up that payment in Quicken *before* you start setting up the loan. Use the techniques laid out in Chapter 6 to create the online repeating payment, entering the amount of your monthly payment as its amount.

To begin tracking a loan, locate your loan records, then open the Activities menu and choose **Loans**. You'll see the View Loans window, shown in Figure 8.15.

Set up the loan and the associated liability account as follows:

1. Click the **New** button on the View Loans button bar. Quicken presents a familiar EasyStep window, this time arranged to help you set up the loan (Figure 8.16). Step through the panels one at a time, supplying the information Quicken requests and clicking the **Next** button to move on. There are quite a few panels to work through, but the information required is fairly basic and should be readily available on your loan documents.

173

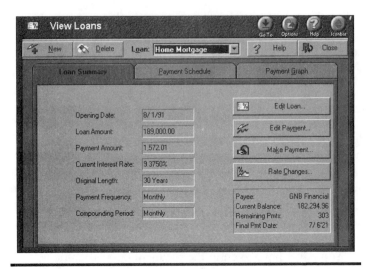

Figure 8.15 Use this window to set up new loans in Quicken and display information about loans you've previously set up.

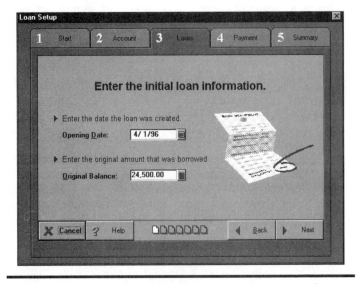

Figure 8.16 Let Quicken walk you through the process of setting up a new loan in this window.

2. When you've completed the final EasyStep window, click **Done**. Quicken creates the new liability account if necessary and displays the Set Up Loan Payment window, shown in Figure 8.17. The amounts in the first two fields have been filled in based on your earlier entries during the EasyStep process.

3. Complete the top portion of the Set Up Loan Payment window. If you're required to pay impounds for items such as insurance along with the loan payment itself, click the **Edit** button at the line labeled *Other amounts in payment*. The standard Splits window appears, where you can enter the amount of your payment that goes for each impound on a separate line. When you close the Splits window, Quicken adds these impounds to the amount at Principal and Interest, showing the total payment you must make each month.

175

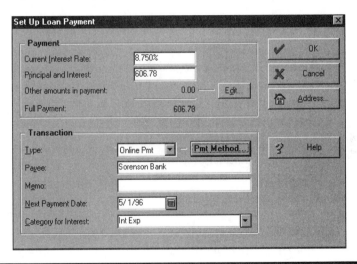

Figure 8.17 Quicken helps you set up your loan payment in this window.

4. Now it's on to the Transaction section of the window. In the Type field, select the type of payment you want Quicken to make: **Payment** (for a plain register transaction), **Print Check**, or **Online Pmt**. Then click the **Pmt Method** button to display the secondary box shown in Figure 8.18.

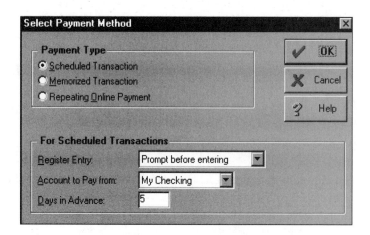

Figure 8.18 The Method of Payment box.

5. Here, choose the way you want Quicken to make your payments:

   • *memorized transaction,* if you want to manually insert the transaction in your checking account each time the payment is due, or assign the memorized transaction to a transaction group that Quicken enters for you each month (see Chapter 6 for details on memorized transactions and transaction groups).

   • *scheduled transaction,* if you want Quicken to add it to your account for you as an individual transaction. If you select this option, you must also fill in the details requested in the lower part of the box (see the section on scheduled transactions in Chapter 6 if you need help with these).

   • *online repeating payment,* if you want to have the bank pay the bill for you each month automatically, without any further input from you. Choose the existing repeating payment for your loan from the drop-down list. If you haven't already set up a corresponding online repeating payment, you won't be able to select this choice.

6. Click **OK** in the Method of Payment box to return to the Set Up Loan Payment box. Enter the payee—the name of the lender—

in the next field. If you specified an online payment, you'll be asked to set up the payee for online payments if you haven't already done so. After typing in a memo, enter the date your next payment is due and select the category you want to assign to the interest portion of your loan payments.

7. Click **OK** to finish the set up process. You're returned to the View Loan window, which now displays a summary of the loan details.

Making Payments on an Amortized Loan

After you've set up an amortized loan, you use the payment transaction created during the setup process to pay the loan and record the fact in Quicken each month. If you created the payment as a memorized transaction, you can use QuickFill to plop it into your account at the appropriate time.

If you created it as a scheduled transaction or added it to a transaction group, Quicken will place it into your account for you—perhaps asking your permission first—at the appointed time. In this case, before Quicken actually enters the transaction in your account, you'll be given an opportunity to change the amounts you're paying for principal and interest. If you've included a prepayment of principal with your monthly check, you enter these extra funds in this window. When you're satisfied with the amounts, click **OK**.

NOTE

With any of the above payment methods, you'll then have to see that the payment is sent to the lender, either by sending an online payment, or by writing and mailing a check.

If you created the payment as an online repeating transaction, Quicken automatically creates a transaction representing the payment at the correct time each month. You don't have to do anything else, since the bank pays the bill without further instruction from you.

In any case, the payment transaction should be entered in your checking account (where the money for the payment came from). When it gets there, Quicken simultaneously creates a parallel transfer transaction in the loan liability account in the amount of the principal you've just paid. It also recalculates the loan balance and adjusts the schedule to reflect the new balance.

Summary

In this chapter you've surveyed more bread-and-butter techniques you'll need for monitoring everyday financial activity with Quicken. You've learned about the different types of Quicken accounts and how to record transfers of funds between them, whether you transfer the funds with an online command or old-fashioned withdrawals and deposits. You now know how to keep track of savings accounts, credit cards, and cash with Quicken. And you've learned to set up Quicken accounts to monitor major assets and liabilities like the value of your home and its mortgage. In Chapter 9, you'll pick up the methods—online and otherwise—you need for keeping track of investments in Quicken.

CHAPTER NINE:

Online Investing with Quicken

Using Quicken doesn't you guarantee fat profits on Wall Street, but it can help you keep close tabs on the money you've invested. With *Investor Insight*, a separate program included with Quicken Deluxe, you have immediate online access to all the information you need to guide investment decisions. Quicken itself has online investment-related capabilities—albeit less extensive than those of Investor Insight—and it is well endowed with other tools for managing your investment holdings.

Before we get started, a word of caution is in order: This is the longest and most complex chapter in this book. There's a good reason for this—managing investments is necessarily more complicated than keeping track of a checking account. If you already invest actively, you should find the material here quite basic. But if you're new to investing, don't expect to understand all the concepts immediately.

Managing Investments
Online with Investor Insight

The Investor Insight program included with Quicken doesn't do much by itself. But it becomes a powerful investor's tool when you subscribe to the online Investor Insight service from Intuit, Quicken's publisher.

Once you've registered for the service, you can use Investor Insight and your modem to access a large online library of up-to-date information on stocks and mutual funds. At your command, Investor Insight retrieves current and historical price quotes and late-breaking news on the stocks you're following. Armed with this information, the program can then generate a range of charts and reports that analyze the performance of your investments both individually and in groups.

At this writing, you can choose either of two subscription rates depending on the number of stocks and mutual funds you want to monitor. To get you hooked, Intuit offers a free one-month trial.

Setting up to Use Investor Insight

If you haven't yet installed Investor Insight, do so by running the Setup program on the first Quicken diskette or the Quicken CD-ROM. Run Investor Insight by choosing it in the Quicken group in the Start Menu (Windows 95) or the Program Manager (Windows 3.1). The Investor Insight window appears on your screen, as shown in Figure 9.1.

Investor Insight includes an iconbar much like the one in Quicken, with buttons for activating most major functions. When activated, each of these functions appears in a separate window.

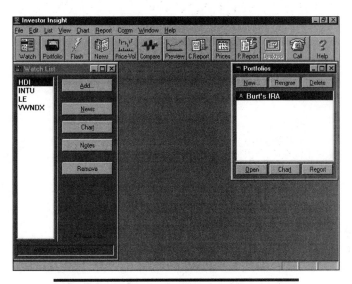

Figure 9.1 The main Investor Insight window.

Signing up for the Investor Insight Service

Investor Insight is a subscription service requiring a monthly fee. Before you can use the service, you have to provide billing information including your name and address as well as the credit card number that will be charged each month. Investor Insight handles the sign-up procedure for you online via your modem.

NOTE

> If you prefer you can wait to sign up with the Investor Insight service until you've customized the watch list to include the securities you want to track—see "Creating Your Personal Watch List," later in this chapter. Once you've changed the watch list, Investor Insight offers you the opportunity to go online and retrieve data for the securities you've added to the list. And if you've never registered before, you'll be given a chance to at that time.

To sign up for Investor Insight:

1. Begin by clicking the **Call** icon on the iconbar, shown here:

2. Just as in Quicken, Investor Insight automatically detects and configures your modem. When this process is complete, you'll see the Set Up Modem window where you can make changes in the unlikely event this is necessary. Click **OK**.

3. Investor Insight displays a small box asking whether you already have a user name and password. When you click **No**, you'll be asked to read the subscription agreement. If you agree to the terms, click **Accept** to proceed.

4. You'll now see the User Registration window (Figure 9.2). Enter the requested information, including your credit card type, number, and expiration date. Investor Insight assigns you a user name based on your full name, but you can type in your own user name if you like. Choose a password, entering it twice to ensure you've typed it correctly.

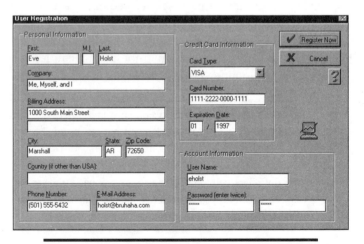

Figure 9.2 Enter billing information in this window.

5. Click **Register Now**. The program calls the Investor Insight service, registering your name, address, and billing information. When the call is complete, you'll see a confirmation message. Click **OK** to confirm your registration.

Familiarizing Yourself with Investor Insight

Investor Insight comes with sample information on several companies. When you first use the program, these securities are already entered in the watch list. Feel free to use the sample data to fiddle around with the program's charting and reporting features.

Like Quicken, Investor Insight includes lots of helpful screens to bring you quickly up to speed. From the Help menu you can choose **Overview** or **Easy Steps** to run through brief tutorials, or **Qcards** to display small windows that automatically explain whatever feature you're working with (If you have the Quicken CD-ROM, QCards are called *Guide Cards,* and have audio text available).

Creating Your Personal Watch List

The heart of Investor Insight is the *watch list,* the list of securities you have chosen to track with the program. When you connect to the online Investor Insight service, the program automatically retrieves price information and news for the securities on your watch list. When you're not online, you can create charts and reports on the securities in the watch list, and use the watch list to select items to include in your custom portfolios and securities indexes.

NOTE

You don't have to own a security to include it in the watch list. Use the watch list for any security you're interested in.

If the watch list isn't already visible, display it by clicking the **Watch** button on the iconbar:

As shown in Figure 9.3, the watch list is a simple list of ticker symbols for the securities it contains. When you click one of the symbols, the full name of the security appears at the bottom of the window.

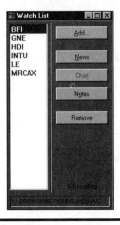

Figure 9.3 The watch list.

Adding Securities to the Watch List

The watch list can accommodate as many securities as you plan to track using Investor Insight. There's just one caveat: the monthly fee you're charged for the service depends on how many securities you're tracking.

To add new items to the watch list, click the **Add** button. You'll see the window shown in Figure 9.4.

The window is empty the first time you open it. Investor Insight asks if you want to build the index files needed to access the comprehensive list of securities that come with the program. Be aware that the process takes 5 minutes or more. If you have the time, give the OK.

Once the index files have been built, the lower part of the Add Securities window lists hundreds of securities with their ticker symbols. To locate the one you want to add, click the corresponding button in the Find By area. Then start typing the name or symbol in the

Type Name field. With each letter you type, Investor Insight jumps to the first security or symbol that matches your entry. When the correct security is highlighted, click **Add** to place it on the watch list (or just double-click the security name).

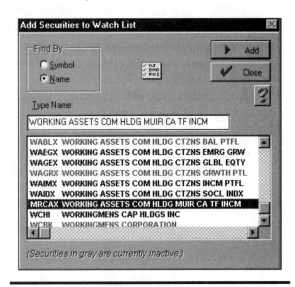

Figure 9.4 The Add Securities to watch list window.

You can add as many securities to the watch list as you like. When you've finished, click **Close** to remove the Add Securities window. You'll be asked when you want to call the Investor Insight service to get information about the securities you've added: now or later. Either way, see "Obtaining Online Information about Your Securities" for details on making an online connection.

Deleting Items from the Watch List

To delete a security from the list, just click its symbol and then click the **Remove** button. You'll probably want to remove some or all of the securities included in the list when you first install Investor Insight.

Obtaining Online Information about Your Securities

Once you have set up your watch list with the securities you want to track, you can go online as often as you like to retrieve information on the stocks and mutual funds on the list. Each time you fire up Investor Insight, your first order of business should be to make an online connection and get the most current prices and news information on your watch list securities.

The first time you go online with Investor Insight after adding a new security to the watch list, the program retrieves price quotes for each market session over the past five years. In addition to the security's current price (as of 15 minutes before), the data includes daily high, low, and closing prices, trading volume, and any stock splits. For individual stocks—but not for mutual funds—Investor Insight also obtains all related news stories and press releases from the past 90 days (sources for this information include the Dow Jones News Service, PR Newswire, and Business Wire).

Each time you connect to the online service from then on, you'll receive price quotes and news stories covering the interval since you last called the service.

Calling the Online Investor Insight Service

To retrieve online information, all you have to do is ready your modem and click the **Call** button on the iconbar. Investor Insight makes the call, retrieves all available information on your securities, and disconnects automatically, displaying a confirmatory message about the call.

If you use Investor Insight heavily, you can set it to call the online service automatically at a set time every day. That way, your daily update on your investments will be ready for you each time you run Investor Insight.

To activate the automated online connection, open the Comm menu and choose **Timer**. In the box that appears (Figure 9.5), click the **Daily** button, then type in the time of day when you want Investor Insight to go online. If you want the program to print incoming news or a personal report at the close of each automatic online session, click the appropriate button.

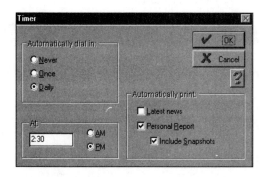

187

Figure 9.5 Activate automatic daily price quotes with this window.

Of course, the automatic connection will work only if the computer and the modem are on at the specified time. If you've requested automated printouts, you must leave your printer on as well.

Viewing Performance Charts

Investor Insight lets you chart the performance and volume activity of the securities on your watch list, individually or in comparison charts. Generating a new chart is as simple as clicking a button and selecting an option or two.

NOTE

Remember, the charts are based on information that is only as current as the last time you connected to the online investment service. Remember to go online and collect the most recent information before displaying the charts.

Price-Volume Charts

The price-volume chart has long been an essential tool of the serious investor, and Investor Insight. Because these charts are so important, Investor Insight gives you a multitude of ways to display them.

The two simplest ways to see a price-volume chart for a particular security (Figure 9.6) are as follows:

Figure 9.6 A price-volume chart.

- Highlight the security's symbol in the watch list, then click **Chart**.

- Click the Price-Vol button on the iconbar: You'll see a window (Figure 9.7) showing miniature charts for all of your watch list securities, allowing you to get a quick sense of how all your holdings are doing. To see the chart for an individual security, just double-click its miniature chart.

In the main part of the an individual security's price-volume window you'll see price information over the selected time period. Unless you change the chart's settings, the chart shows high-low-close information for time periods shorter than one year. Volume data appears graphically along the bottom edge of the chart.

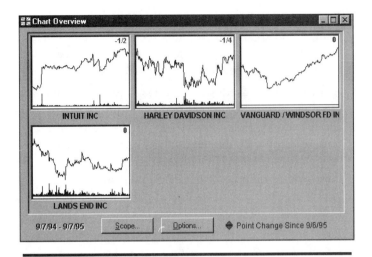

Figure 9.7 This window shows miniature price-volume charts for all your securities.

189

Special events such as news items, stock splits, and your own purchases and sales of the security appear as "Hot Spots," colored dots in the price area. Double-click on a hot spot to see associated details.

To change the time period displayed on the chart, use the drop-down list at the very bottom of the chart window. If none of the preset time periods suit you, select **Custom** and enter the dates you want to view.

Click the **Options** button to add or remove information from the chart. You can display moving price averages for the security, overlay the Dow Jones Industrial and S&P 500 averages on the chart, and add high and low price limit lines. You can also decide which types of Hot Spots are shown on the chart.

Comparative Charts

Investor Insight offers three types of charts for comparing two or more securities, individually or in groups:

- *Percent change charts* show side-by-side bar graphs giving the change in price of each individual security or index in the chart over the chosen period. The securities or indexes with the largest relative price moves are easy to spot.

- *Abnormal volume charts* don't always show "abnormal" volume, but they're intended to help you spot unusual activity in the charted stocks. Side-by-side bars for each item illustrate the trading volume for the selected day relative to the average volume for the quarter. Unusual volume often indicates a shift in the market's opinion of the stock, so it may be wise to see if you've received any news that might explain the change (look in the News window).

- *Burst charts* are often the best way to compare the price performance of two or more securities or indexes. As shown in Figure 9.8, these line charts show the percentage change in value over time of each item.

Figure 9.8 A burst chart.

Preview Charts

Investor Insight comes with historical information for a large number of securities, allowing you to study their performance over the past five years with a "preview" price-volume chart. The idea behind the name is that you can use the chart to decide whether you want to track the security's current performance with Investor Insight.

Display a preview chart by clicking the **Preview** button on the icon-bar:

Click on the stock you want to examine from the list, to display the chart.

> The number of stocks you can evaluate with preview charts depends on which version of Quicken you have. The diskette version comes with historical data for Standard and Poor's 500 stocks, while the CD-ROM version covers the 4000 largest companies.
>
> **NOTE**

Reading News on Watch List Securities

191

To read news and press releases on the securities on your watch list click the **News** button on the iconbar:

Investor Insight displays a window listing all the news stories it has obtained from its online databases (Figure 9.9).

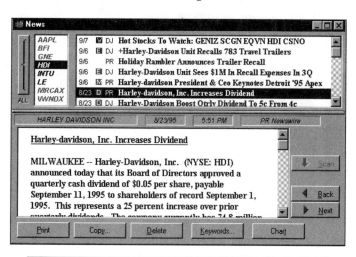

Figure 9.9 Investor Insight displays news in this window.

Use the area at the top left to control which stories appear in the News window. Click the area labeled **All** to see the stories on all your watch list securities. To limit the list to stories on specific securities, click their ticker symbols.

Most of the upper part of the News window is devoted to the titles of the available news items. To read an item, just click on it. The full text appears in the lower half of the window.

Reading the Latest News Flash

To alert you to major events in the general market and your specific stocks, Investor Insight prepares a special news bulletin called a *flash* each time you connect to the online service. As shown in Figure 9.10, the flash report appears in big, bold text that you should have no trouble reading.

192

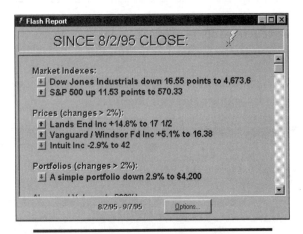

Figure 9.10 An Investor Insight flash report.

To display a flash report, click the button on the iconbar:

Once the report appears, you can specify the items included in this and future flashes by clicking the **Options** button. The Options box also lets you set things up so that Investor Insight displays a flash report immediately after each online session.

Price Reports

To see a simple table listing the current prices of your watch list securities along with the price change over a selected interval, click the Price button on the iconbar: ![Prices] Figure 9.11 shows an example.

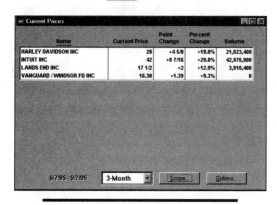

Figure 9.11 A sample Price Report.

193

The controls at the bottom of the window let you select the interval covered in the report and choose other display options. Click **Scope** to specify the securities included in the table and **Options** to select which types of information are displayed.

Personal Reports

Personal reports are a really spiffy Investor Insight feature. They summarize important investment information obtained online in a newsletter-style format, complete with useful comparison charts. You get to control the information that appears on the report, and you can print out the report and peruse it at your leisure.

To generate a personal report, click the **P. Report** button on the iconbar: ![P.Report]

You'll see a window with a mockup of the report as shown in Figure 9.12. You can barely read some of the text, but don't bother squinting—you'll be able to see it better in a moment. First, look at the buttons along the left side of the report window.

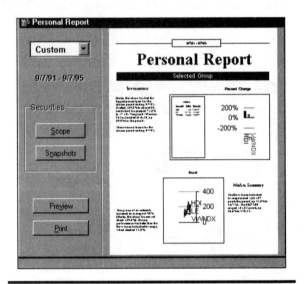

Figure 9.12 Display a personal report in this window.

Set the interval you want the report to cover using the drop-down list at the top left. To limit the report to specific securities, click the **Securities** button and pick the ones you want to see. Use the **Snapshots** button to specify whether the report includes the online news stories Investor Insight has retrieved; otherwise, the report simply summarizes the performance of the securities over the selected period.

To view the report on your screen, click the **Preview** button. You'll now be able to zoom in to read the text comfortably. If you want a printed copy, click the **Print** button on either the main report window or from the preview.

Company Reports

If you're willing to pay for the privilege (about $5), you can use Investor Insight to obtain detailed investment reports on any stock you're interested in. Similar to the reports you might get from a stock broker or investment research firm, these "company reports" summarize the company's product line, market position, and financial performance. In addition, you get a tabulation of the buy/sell/hold ratings of stock market analysts (although the report doesn't say which analysts are surveyed).

To obtain a company report, first make sure you've added the security to your watch list. Then click the **C. Report** button on the iconbar:

Proceed through two small boxes as follows: Click the **Order** button, choose the security you want from the list, and then click **Order** in the second box. When you close the box, Investor Insight asks whether you want to call the online service now to obtain the report.

If you mistakenly order a report you don't really want, delete the order in the Outbox. Open the Comm menu, click **Outbox**, then highlight the order in the list and click **Delete**.

Using Portfolios to Track Groups of Securities

In Investor Insight, a *portfolio* is a set of individual securities that you wish to track as a group. The portfolio can include investment cash as well.

In a typical scenario, you might create one portfolio for short- and medium-term investments and another for the long-term holdings you've earmarked for retirement. You might also have one or more portfolios to follow securities that you don't actually own, and use them to see whether the recommendations of an investment newsletter match the claims.

Use the Portfolios window to create, modify, and analyze Investor Insight portfolios. To display the window (Figure 9.13), click the **Portfolio** button on the iconbar:

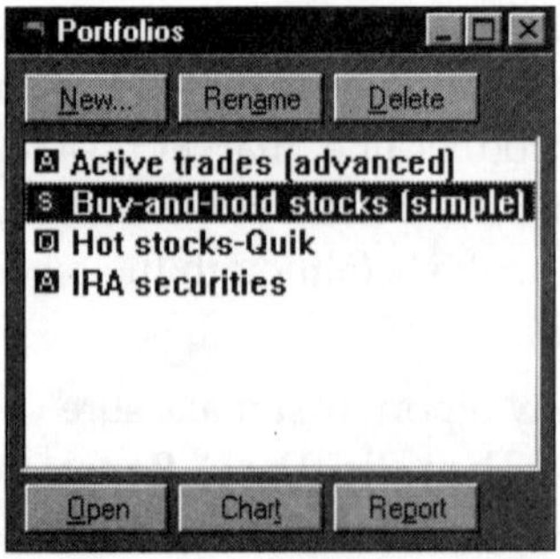

HOME BANKING WITH QUICKEN

Figure 9.13 The Portfolios window.

Types of Portfolios

Investor Insight lets you create three different types of portfolios: simple, advanced, and Quicken.

- *Simple portfolios,* as you would expect, are the easiest to use, but provide less information than the other types. With a simple portfolio, you can compare the total value of the portfolio securities with their original purchase price (See Figure 9.14).

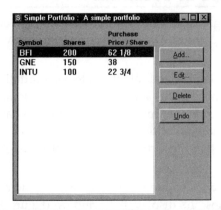

Figure 9.14 The main window for a simple portfolio.

On the other hand, you can't use it to record separate sales and purchases of the same security, nor can you list cash adjustments such as dividend income or commissions. And although a simple portfolio allows you to compare the listed purchase price of your holdings against historical data, such comparisons may not be valid—since the portfolio doesn't "know" when you bought a given security, you may not have owned the security, or the same number of shares, on the past date in question.

- *Advanced portfolios* give you a more accurate picture of the total value of your investments. They let you enter individual cash transactions covering dividend income and commissions (See Figure 9.15). You can also record multiple purchases and sales of the same security in one advanced portfolio, allowing you to make sophisticated performance computations such as time-weighted return. Because advanced portfolios record the date of each transaction, Investor Insight can calculate and display the actual portfolio value for any day.

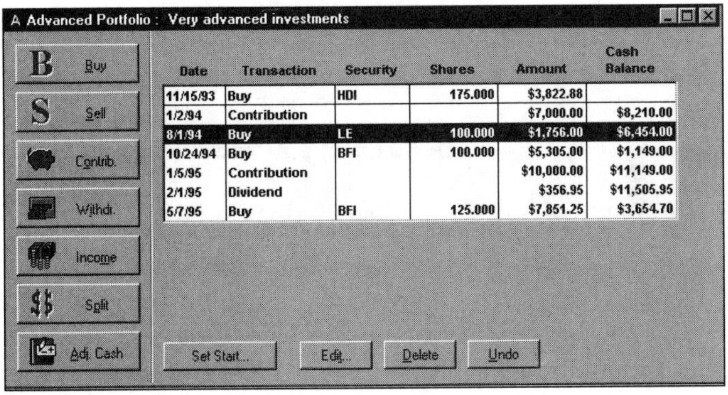

Figure 9.15 The window for a sample advanced portfolio.

- *Quicken portfolios* are similar to advanced portfolios, except that the information they contain comes directly from Quicken investment accounts (investment accounts are covered later in this chapter). Because the transactions in these portfolios come from your Quicken records, you can't modify them in Investor

Insight. However, you can still generate Investor Insight charts and reports based on the data in these portfolios.

Portfolio Charts and Reports

To view a portfolio chart, highlight the portfolio in the Portfolios window and click **Chart**. You'll see the little window shown in Figure 9.16.

Figure 9.16 Choose the type of portfolio chart in this window.

Here, select the type of portfolio chart you want to see:

- *Holdings charts* use a pie chart format to illustrate the distribution of the portfolio's total value among the various securities in the portfolio.

- *Relative value charts* compare the value of each portfolio security in order starting with the most valuable holding. Each three-dimensional bar shows both the current and the original value of the security.

- *Portfolio value charts* simply give the dollar value for the portfolio as a whole for every date in the chosen interval.

- *Portfolio vs. Dow Jones* charts compare the portfolio's performance against that of the Dow Jones Industrial Average over the specified time period.

Sending and Receiving E-Mail

Investor Insight lets you exchange *e-mail* (electronic mail) with the online Investor Insight service. When you inquire about services, offer suggestions, or register complaints via an e-mail message, you'll receive an online answer within two working days.

To create an e-mail message, open the Comm menu and click **Write E-mail**. In the window that appears (Figure 9.17), type the subject of your message and the message itself. If you have a lot to say, you can attach a file prepared in your word processor and saved in plain text (ASCII) format.

199

Figure 9.17 Use this window to compose e-mail
messages to the Investor Insight service.

Each time you call the online service with Investor Insight the program picks up any replies or other messages addressed to you. To read your mail, open the Comm menu and click **Inbox**. The Inbox window lists the mail items you've received. You can read an item by clicking it in the list. If you want to reply to the message, click the **Reply** button. When you've read and digested the message, click **Delete** to remove it from the list.

The Inbox also lists company reports you have ordered and received. To read a report, select it in the list and click **View**.

TIP

Using Quicken Investment Accounts

Independent of Investor Insight, Quicken itself offers a complete system for keeping track of investments such as stocks, bonds, and mutual funds. Using Quicken's investment accounts, you can easily record purchases and sales of securities and track their value as market prices change. And Quicken can even retrieve stock price quotes online via its portfolio update feature.

Although they have many similar features, Quicken and Investor Insight complement one another and work well together. Investor Insight's key strength, of course, is its ability to retrieve more detailed online information as often as you like. In addition, its price-volume and comparison charts are more useful than Quicken graphs in helping you make investment decisions. And they are better for monitoring investments that don't have ticker symbols, such as precious metals, commodities, and real estate investment trust shares.

On the other hand, Quicken's investment accounts let you monitor the impact of your investments on your overall financial situation, something you can't do with Investor Insight. They also allow more precise accounting of investment transactions.

Fortunately, you can set up the two programs to transfer information back and forth automatically. After you transfer a Quicken investment account to Investor Insight as a Quicken portfolio, the portfolio automatically reflects all new transactions in the account. Likewise, price information obtained online by Investor Insight will automatically be added to your Quicken investment accounts.

Understanding Investment Accounts

Quicken investment accounts are tailor-made for securities such as stocks, bonds, and shares of mutual funds or real estate trusts, whose prices vary frequently. Commodities that have a variable price per unit, such as precious metals, fall into this category as well. But you can also use Quicken investment accounts to track brokerage accounts and similar conglomerations of investments that may include cash or other fixed-price instruments in addition to stocks, bonds, and the like.

200

On the other hand, you wouldn't ordinarily use an investment account to keep track of a certificate of deposit (CD), a money market fund, or any other investment whose price—or price per share—remains constant. Instead, use a standard Quicken bank (savings) account for such holdings.

Setting up an Investment Account

By now you're familiar with the Quicken procedures required to activate a new account. Beginning in the Account List window, click **New**. Next, click the **Investment** button in the New Accounts box. Proceed by filling in the requested information as Quicken walks you through the EasyStep panels for new investment accounts.

NOTE

You don't enter a dollar balance for the account value when you set up an investment account. Instead, after creating the account, you add the necessary transactions to bring the balance into line with that of your real investment portfolio. We'll discuss the procedures in later sections of the chapter.

After entering a name and description for the account, you'll be asked whether you're using the account to track a single mutual fund. Quicken offers two subtypes of investment accounts, the "regular" kind and a special type for individual mutual funds. Ordinary investment accounts allow you to keep track of a cash balance in the account as you sell shares, receive dividends or interest payments. And they let you follow as many separate securities of any type—including mutual funds—as you'd like in the same account. However, an ordinary investment account won't tell you how many shares you own of each security.

By contrast, a mutual fund investment account accepts entries for only one mutual fund. You can't accumulate cash in the account, but this can be a plus—cash transfers to and from these accounts are automatic as you buy and sell shares. And you always get to see the total number of shares you own of the mutual fund from the account register.

Once you've answered the mutual fund account question, Quicken next asks whether you want to link the new account to a specific checking account. If you choose **No**, the investment account balance reflects investment cash as well as the value of your noncash investments.

If you choose **Yes**, the linked checking account will monitor the balance of a brokerage account where you keep uninvested cash, while the investment account tracks the dollar value of your securities. All transactions involving cash are automatically set up as transfer transactions in both accounts (see Chapter 8 for a discussion of transfers in Quicken). If you do choose **Yes**, Quicken will ask whether you want to link the investment account to a new bank account or one that you've previously created.

TIP

To include a linked checking account in an investment income report, you'll have to customize the report, selecting the account by name in the Accounts tab of the Customize Report window.

The next EasyStep panel asks whether you will be using the account to track tax deferred investments such as an IRA. If you choose **Yes**, Quicken excludes the account from tax reports.

In the next panel you're asked a related question: whether to assign tax schedules to transfer transactions recorded in this account. Be sure to choose **Yes** if you're setting up an account for tax deferred investments. If you do, the next panel lets you select a form and line number from your federal tax return for transfers in and out of the account. For example, transfers into an IRA account from your other accounts should be linked to the line on form 1040 for that purpose, while withdrawals would be linked to the "other income" line (you've already paid social security taxes on the funds).

Complete the account setup by entering miscellaneous information about the account if you like. When you click **Done**, the account appears in the Account List window.

NOTE

When you set up your first investment account, Quicken automatically adds a set of investment-related categories to your file for use with miscellaneous investment-related transactions you record your Quicken accounts. These categories are all named with an initial underscore, as in _IntExp, so they appear together in the category list.

Entering Stock Transactions

You can enter transactions into investment accounts in two ways: directly into the register or on a special "form," a small window containing all the same fields as those that appear in the register.

You must identify the type of each investment transaction by assigning it an "action" designation (the Action field corresponds to the Num field in a bank account register). There are many possible actions to choose from, and many of the abbreviations that appear in the register are somewhat cryptic. Table 9.1, which lists and defines the actions, should make selecting the correct one a bit easier.

Table 9.1 Stock Transactions

Action List Types	Action Items	Explanation
Add/Remove Shares	ShrsIn	Add shares without accounting for cash used.
	ShrsOut	Remove shares without accounting for proceeds.
Buy shares	Buy	Shares purchased with cash in investment acct.
	BuyX	Shares purchased w/cash transferred from another acct.
Capital gain distributions	CGLong	Long-term capital gains.
	CGLongX	Long-term capital gains transferred to another account.
	CGSh	Short-term capital gains.

Table 9.1 (continued)

Action List Types	Action Items	Explanation
	CGShortX	Short-term capital gains transferred to another account.
Dividends	Div	Dividend income.
	DivX	Dividend income transferred to another account.
Interest	IntInc	Interest income.
	MargInt	Interest paid on margin loan (broker loan).
Other transactions	MiscExp	Miscellaneous expense.
	MiscInc	Miscellaneous income item.
	Reminder	Used to remind you to enter a transfer later and to note a change in company name.
	RtrnCap	Cash received from return of capital.
	StkSplt	Change in number of shares owned due to stock split.
Reinvest	ReinvDiv	Additional shares purchased with dividend or income distribution.
	ReinvLg	Additional shares purchased with long-term capital gains distribution.
	ReinvSh	Additional shares purchased with short-term capital gains distribution.
Sell Shares	Sell	Sell shares, with income from sale left in current investment account.
	SellX	Sell shares, transferring income to another account.
Transfer Cash	Xin	Transfer cash to investment account from another account.
	Xout	Transfer cash from investment account to another account.

Use the sample transactions below to familiarize yourself with the investment register. The samples cover the most common types of investment transactions. Some of the fields in each sample are empty, either because the field doesn't pertain to that type of transaction, or because Quicken calculates the correct value for you from the other entries.

The first sample transaction records the shares of a stock you already owned at the time you started the investment account:

Date	5/1/96
Action	ShrsIn
Security	Apple Computer
Price	40 1/4
Shares	150
Amount	
Commission	

The second sample transaction is a new purchase of additional shares of the same security, bought with cash "parked" in this investment account:

Date	5/15/96
Action	Buy
Security	Apple Computer
Price	48 3/8
Shares	50
Amount	
Commission	75

The third sample transaction represents a dividend you received on your stock holdings:

Date	6/5/96
Action	Div
Security	Apple Computer

Price	
Shares	
Amount	$22.50
Commission	

The fourth and final of our sample stock transactions records a sale of half of your imaginary holdings:

Date	9/20/96
Action	Sell
Security	Apple Computer
Price	59 7/8
Shares	100
Amount	
Commission	120

Recording Shares You Already Own: The First Sample Transaction

Enter the first transaction directly in the register. After correcting the date, make an entry in the Action field by typing it in, allowing Quickfill to complete the entry for you. If you need more information about the action choices, press **F1** from the Action field to call up the Help menu on that topic.

Since the transaction you're entering represents shares that you already owned on the date indicated, you should enter **ShrsIn** rather than Buy as the action for this transaction. The entry ShrsIn tells Quicken not to require a source of cash for the shares you're adding to the account. In this case, since two action items begin with Shrs, it's probably quickest to choose the **ShrsIn** item from the list rather than typing it in with Quickfill's help.

Setting up Securities

In the next field, type the name of the security, **Apple Computer**, and press **Tab**. Quicken will display the Set Up Security dialog box (see

Figure 9.18). You'll see this dialog box every time you add a new security to an investment account.

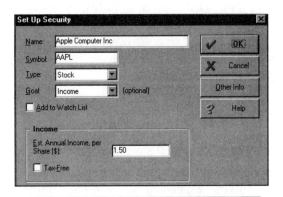

Figure 9.18 The Set Up Security dialog box.

207

You can also add securities to your account or edit existing securities using the Security list. To access the list, open the Lists menu and click **Security**.

NOTE

In the Set Up Security box, Quicken has already filled in the Name field with your entry, but you can edit this if necessary. Then enter the security's ticker symbol as printed in newspaper stock tables—it's *AAPL* for Apple Computer. If you plan to use your Quicken account in Investor Insight, it's vital that you enter the ticker symbol correctly.

In the Type field, select the type of security you're working with, **Stock**, from the drop-down list. The entry in the Type field is important, since Quicken groups securities by type in the Portfolio View window for easier entry of share prices, and since you can make focused reports covering only specific types of securities.

Quicken comes with four security types (*Stock, Bond, CD,* and *Mutual Fund*) and you can set up 12 other custom types. To modify the list of security types, open the Lists menu and click **Security Type**.

TIP

The Goal field is for an entry that describes your purpose in buying the security. Again, make your selection of a goal from the drop-down list. The goals supplied by Quicken include generic objectives such as growth and incomes, but you're free to create a Tahiti vacation goal if you'd like (to create a new goal, open the Lists menu and click **Investment Goal**). Later, you can generate reports and graphs that track your investments by goal.

Check the **Add to watch list** box if you want to place the new security on the Quicken watch list (*not* the watch list in Investor Insight). In Quicken, the watch list is used to follow securities you're interested in even if they aren't listed in any investment account transactions.

Finally, if you want to keep track of how well the investment performs relative to your expectations, fill in the Annual Income field with the per-share earnings you expect. If you enter an amount here, Quicken will use it to calculate measurements such as investment yield in the Portfolio View window.

208

Continuing the Register Transaction

After completing the Set Up Security dialog box, choose **OK** to return to the register. In the next field, Price, type in the security's price per share on the date of the transaction. The price of the first sample entry includes a fraction, which you must enter by leaving a space after the dollar amount—type **40 1/4**. As long as the price you enter follows this format, Quicken will display its calculation in the Amount field in the same format.

NOTE

If you'd prefer, you can enter securities prices as dollars and cents, as in **$40.25**. You can control the way Quicken displays the price—as a fraction or a decimal number—by using the security list to edit the security type.

Move to the Shares field by pressing **Tab**. When you enter the number of shares owned as of this transaction date, Quicken automatically calculates the total value of all your shares in the Amount field. To complete the entry, move to the Memo field and type in a brief comment about this transaction. Then record the transaction.

Recording a Purchase of New Shares: The Second Sample Transaction

The second sample transaction is a new purchase of additional shares of the same security, bought with cash "parked" in this investment account. For transactions of this type, the entry in the Action field should be **Buy**. But this time, instead of typing the transaction directly into the register, you'll enter the information in an investment transaction "form," a separate dialog box.

Using Forms to Enter Transactions

To display a transaction entry form, click the **Action** button at the top of the account window and choose the action you want. You'll see the window shown in Figure 9.19.

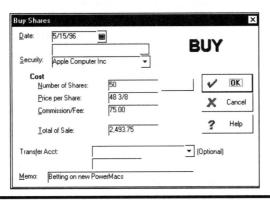

Figure 9.19 The entry form for a Buy transaction.

NOTE

You may notice that the menu you see doesn't list every possible action available in the Action field's drop-down list (Table 9.1). That's because some of the menu choices cover more than one action, depending on the entries you make in the transaction form. The Buy form used in this transaction for example can create both Buy and BuyX transactions.

Fill in the transaction details using the sample information above. In the security field, instead of typing in the full name again, you can use Quickfill or choose the name from the drop-down list. Enter the price per share, number of shares, and the commission amount for the transaction. Quicken calculates the total amount of the transaction for you.

Down at the bottom of the window, type in a memo if you like. Ignore the Transfer Acct field for now—you use it when you buy shares with money from another account (BuyX transactions). Choose **OK** to record the transaction and to return to the register.

Recording a Dividend: The Third Sample Transaction

The third sample transaction records dividend income on your investment. You can enter the transaction with either of the two methods you've already learned. Either way, begin by entering the date and then entering **Div** in the Action field. In the register, when you leave the Security field the cursor will jump all the way over to the Amount field. Again, dividend transactions have blank columns where you entered price and share information in the earlier transactions, and Quicken won't accept entries there. To enter the transaction on a form, click **Edit** and choose **Open Transaction Form**.

Recording a Stock Sale: The Fourth Sample Transaction

The final sample transaction covers a sale of part of your Apple holdings. Again, you can enter this transaction either by typing it directly into the register, or by entering **Sell** in the Action field and then displaying the corresponding form.

Selling these shares brings up an accounting question: Since you bought the stock on two separate occasions—in two different *lots*—from which lot do you want to sell shares? The answer has tax implications.

Tracking Separate Lots of the Same Security

For example, suppose you've held the first lot for longer than a year but the second lot only three months. Selling shares of the first lot gives you a long-term capital gain, taxed at lower rates than the short-term gain you'd realize on sales of the second lot.

Or what if you paid twice as much per share for the first lot as the second? If the price has since rebounded from its bottom but is still below what you originally paid, you can sell shares of the first lot at a capital loss, offsetting profits in other securities that would otherwise be taxed. If you sell from the second lot instead, you'll pay additional capital gains taxes on those shares.

Quicken automatically keeps track of separate lots of the same security and offers you a chance to indicate which lot you used when you record a sale of that stock, bond, and so on. If you enter the **Sell** transaction in the register, Quicken asks whether you want to identify the lot the shares came from when you record the transaction. If you use a form to record the transaction, you'll see a button labeled **Lots**.

211

To tell Quicken which lot to use for the sale, choose **Yes** to Quicken's question or click the **Lots** button in the Sell Shares window. You'll see a special window for identifying the source of the shares you sold (Figure 9.20).

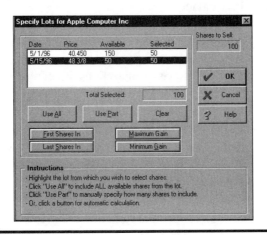

Figure 9.20 Identify the lot you're selling in this window.

The main section of the window lists all available lots of the security, showing you when you bought each lot, how much you paid, and how many shares you now hold. At the top right, it displays the number of shares you entered as sold in the previous window.

Use the buttons below the list to choose shares from the available lots for the sale. You can have Quicken select shares meeting common criteria for you with the **First Shares In**, **First Shares Out**, **Maximum Gain**, and **Minimum Gain** buttons. To choose shares yourself, highlight a lot and click one of the following buttons: Use **All** to select all available shares; or use **Part** to type in the number of shares from that lot you want to select.

Adjusting Cash and Share Balances

As you know, you don't enter a dollar value for an investment account when you create the account. At this point, if you have entered the sample transactions as printed, Quicken displays a significant negative cash balance, reflecting the amount you spent on new investment purchases subtracted from your meager dividend earnings and what you earned from when you sold some of your holdings of Apple stock. Actually, your account would have contained more than enough cash to cover the original purchase, and it should now be showing a positive balance.

Under such circumstances, you have two choices for correcting the account balance:

- You can enter *all* past transactions involving the securities you're tracking in the account. In addition to purchases and sales of securities, you would need to enter every transaction in which cash moved into or out of the account.

- An easier alternative is to have Quicken update the cash value of the account to that of your actual holdings, including any uninvested cash.

To take the latter course, open the Activities menu and choose **Update Balances —> Update Cash Balance**. In the dialog box that appears

(Figure 9.21), enter the current actual cash balance in the account. Change the date to one prior to your first buy or sell transaction. When you choose **OK**, Quicken creates a special transaction adding or subtracting cash so that the current balance is correct.

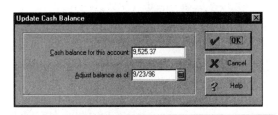

Figure 9.21 Update the balance in your investment account with this dialog box.

Similarly, you can have Quicken reset the number of shares of any given security the account holds. Again, start from the Activities menu. Choose **Update Balances —> Update Share Balance**. In the window, enter the date on which you want Quicken to make the adjustment. In the next field, type the name of the security whose share balance you'd like to change. Finally, enter the total number of shares of the chosen security that should be in your account after the adjustment (don't enter the number of shares you want to add or subtract—Quicken does the math for you). Then choose **OK**.

213

Tracking Your Investments in Quicken

Once you've set up your investment accounts, you can use them to monitor the health of your investments on a regular basis and to prepare reports whenever you need them for tax purposes or portfolio analysis.

Monitoring Market Value in the Register

At the lower-right corner of the Investment Account window, Quicken lists two items of bottom-line importance: the dollar amount of the cash currently in your account (Ending Cash Bal) and the current market value of the entire account, including the cash balance

(Market Value). If your cash balance is zero, the market value displayed represents the amount you would realize if you sold the investments in your account. If you do have cash in the account, you must subtract the cash balance from the market value shown to obtain the value of your securities or other investments.

Of course, the accuracy of the information Quicken displays on these two lines or provides in reports and graphs depends on how complete and up-to-date you keep your investment accounts. Whenever a significant change in your portfolio takes place, you'll want to record the new information by adding corresponding transactions to your accounts (see "Recording New Transactions") or by updating the market prices of your holdings (as described later, in "Updating Market Prices").

Using Portfolio View

Portfolio View provides a central control panel for managing your investments. The Portfolio View window lists any combination of securities from any or all your investment accounts on a selected date. Again, you open the Portfolio View window by clicking its button on the iconbar or on the toolbar of any investment account.

The main section of the Portfolio View window lists your investment holdings by type (stocks, bonds, and so on), organizing them alphabetically within these groups. For each security, the table shows its most recent price available as of the date at the top of the window, the direction of price change since the last previous recorded price, and information about the market value and performance of the investment. If Quicken has "estimated" the market price, as indicated by a small *e* at the right of the Mkt Price column, this means there is no Buy or Sell transaction for that date.

The information in the last three columns depends on which "view" you've chosen. At the top-right corner of the window, the drop-down list labeled *Views* lets you select from several built-in profiles and two custom ones that you can build yourself. When you select a view, the headings and data in the last three columns change accordingly.

Below the list of individual investments, Quicken figures your overall percentage gain or loss and totals the market value of all the investments shown.

Quicken fills in all this information for you. However, you can change one entry yourself: the market price per share. That's how you update your account to bring it in line with the current prices of your real-life investments.

Buttons and Controls on the Portfolio View Window

The portfolio View window is replete with buttons and other controls. Here's an outline of what they do:

- *Action*: This button works different here than it does in an investment account register—it lets you enter new investment transactions via a form. Click the button to display a menu of investment actions (**Buy, Sell**, and so forth). When you select an action the corresponding form appears. If you've set portfolio view to display multiple accounts, be sure to select the account where you want to record the transaction as you complete the form.

- *Update*: With your modem ready, click this button to get online price quotes for all the securities on your security list via the Portfolio Price Update service from Intuit, Quicken's publisher. To use this service successfully, you must first assign the correct ticker symbol to each security on the list. Quicken dials the online service and retrieves each security's last price, the price change, and when available, high, low, and volume data. After three free price updates, you'll be asked to sign up for the service, providing address and billing information.

- *Register*: When Portfolio View displays securities from a single investment account, you can click here to move directly to that account's register. The button doesn't work if the Portfolio View window shows more than one account.

- *Options*: Click here to open a window offering many options for the Portfolio View display. You can select which accounts and

215

securities appear in the window, specify the interval for return calculations, and set up customized views showing the types of information you specify.

- *Report*: To display a report showing all transactions for a particular investment, highlight the security in the Portfolio View window, then click the **Report** button. You can display the same report by simply double-clicking over the chosen security.

- *Close*: This button closes the Portfolio View window.

- *Prices for Date*: Click here to set the date shown on the Portfolio View window.

- *Account drop-down list*: Select the account to display from the drop-down list at the middle of the window, just below the toolbar.

- *Views drop-down list*: Choose the "view" you want to display in the Portfolio View window from the drop-down list. The list includes both custom views you can create with the Options window.

- *Graph*: At the left of the Portfolio View window just below the main listing of securities, this button generates a graph of the selected security's price history.

- *Price*: Select a security in the Portfolio View window and click on this button to display the history of daily prices you've recorded in Quicken (Figure 9.22). Price Information you retrieve with online Portfolio Price Updates appears in this window. To add a price manually, click the **New** button in the Price History window (alternatively, you can just type in the new price in the Mkt Price column in the main Portfolio View window).

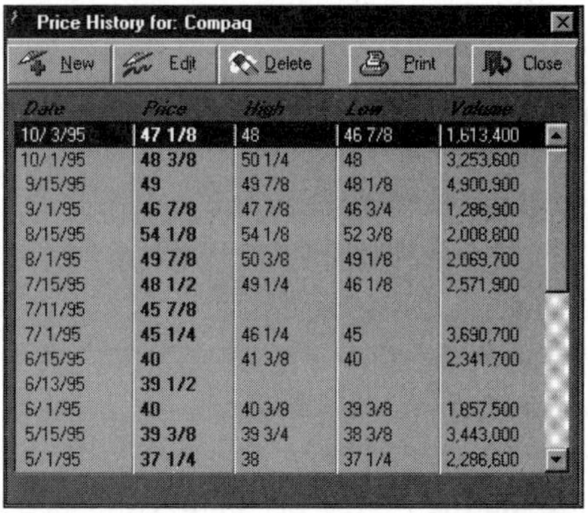

Date	Price	High	Low	Volume
10/3/95	47 1/8	48	46 7/8	1,613,400
10/1/95	48 3/8	50 1/4	48	3,253,600
9/15/95	49	49 7/8	48 1/8	4,900,900
9/1/95	46 7/8	47 7/8	46 3/4	1,286,900
8/15/95	54 1/8	54 1/8	52 3/8	2,008,800
8/1/95	49 7/8	50 3/8	49 1/8	2,069,700
7/15/95	48 1/2	49 1/4	46 1/8	2,571,900
7/11/95	45 7/8			
7/1/95	45 1/4	46 1/4	45	3,690,700
6/15/95	40	41 3/8	40	2,341,700
6/13/95	39 1/2			
6/1/95	40	40 3/8	39 3/8	1,857,500
5/15/95	39 3/8	39 3/4	38 3/8	3,443,000
5/1/95	37 1/4	38	37 1/4	2,286,600

Figure 9.22 Quicken's Price History window.

Using Quicken and Investor Insight Together

If you've decided to monitor your investments with Quicken, you don't have to give up the online capabilities of Investor Insight—and you don't have to retype all your investment transactions, either. The two programs are designed to work hand in hand with a minimum of effort on your part.

Working with Quicken Portfolios in Investor Insight

If you rely on Quicken to keep track of your overall financial status, you will want to create accounts for your investments and keep them up to date as market conditions change. Besides, even if you wanted to rely exclusively on Investor Insight for investment management, you may not be able to, since the latter program can't track commodities, bonds, and other investments not listed on the major stock exchanges.

Fortunately, you can use Quicken to enter your investment transactions and then transfer the securities to Investor Insight (at least those that the latter program can track). Once Investor Insight has created a "Quicken portfolio" in this way, a click of the mouse mirrors any new transactions you enter in Quicken in the portfolio.

For good results in Investor Insight, first be sure you've assigned the correct ticker symbol to each security in your Quicken investment account. As it adds the Quicken information to its own records, Investor Insight places each security with a valid ticker symbol onto your watch list—but not those with invalid symbols.

After the information from a Quicken account has been added, Investor Insight lists it in the Portfolios window. A small *Q* beside the name is your clue that this is a Quicken portfolio. Since the information comes from a linked Quicken account, you can't change its name or modify the transactions it contains. But you can analyze the securities in the portfolio with Investor Insight charts and reports.

Here's how to create an Investor Insight portfolio linked to a Quicken investment account:

1. In Investor Insight, open the File menu and click **Get Quicken Investments**. Investor Insight reads investment account information from the Quicken file you're currently using (or the last one you used, if Quicken isn't currently running).

2. If the Quicken file contains securities with missing or invalid ticker symbols, you'll be warned about this and given a chance to stop the procedure. Unless you know that the securities in question don't have ticker symbols, you should stop at this point and correct the problem. (In Investor Insight, use the **Add** button in the Watch List window to display a list of securities and their symbols. Locate the correct symbol, write it down, then return to Quicken. There, edit the security in the security list, adding the correct symbol).

3. When Investor Insight displays the Get Quicken Accounts window, pick out the investment accounts you want to add as Quicken portfolios in Investor Insight. Click **Get Data**.

4. Investor Insight retrieves the account information from Quicken, displaying a message box when the job is through. When you click **OK** you'll see the Quicken account names in the Investor Insight Portfolios window.

Examine the new Quicken portfolio by highlighting it and clicking **Open**. You'll see a simple listing of the transactions from the Quicken account. Note that the two programs use similar but somewhat different schemes for identifying transaction types.

Using Investor Insight Price Histories in Quicken

Quicken can add price information obtained by Investor Insight to the price history of any chosen security. Here's how to bring this information into Quicken:

1. Starting from Portfolio View, click over the chosen security with the *right* mouse button.

2. In the menu pop-up shortcuts menu, click **Import Historical Prices**.

3. A small window appears in which you can indicate how far back in time Quicken should get price quotes (up to five years) and with what frequency (daily, weekly, or monthly). Click **OK** to retrieve the price information.

To verify that the Investor Insight prices have been added to Quicken, highlight the security in Portfolio View and click the **Prices** button to see the price history.

Using Investor Insight Stock Quotes in Quicken

As Investor Insight retrieves new price quotes they will automatically be added to Quicken, provided one condition is met: *each security must have been assigned the correct ticker symbol in Quicken*. If necessary, use the Quicken security list to add or correct the symbols for all the securities on your Investor Insight watch list.

Only the most recently retrieved quotes are transferred to Quicken automatically. To keep your Quicken records as current as possible, you should run Quicken after each online session with Investor Insight. If you miss a quote, you can always use the procedure outlined in the previous session to retrieve it manually.

Summary

That completes your tour of the investment management features of Quicken and Investor Insight. You've learned to use Investor Insight to retrieve online stock quotes, historical price information, news stories and press releases, and to put this information to work in informative charts and reports. In Quicken, you now know how to create investment accounts, record all kinds of investment-related transactions, and obtain price quotes via Quicken's own online capabilities. Finally, you've become acquainted with techniques you can use to share information between the two programs, allowing you to take advantage of each one's strengths without duplication of effort.

CHAPTER TEN:

Building Net Worth with Quicken

Banking online with Quicken is a great way to streamline the hassles involved in keeping your day-to-day banking records and paying your bills. When all is said and done, though, financial records themselves aren't very exciting. But they can give you a real charge once you see how they can help you boost your bottom line.

Fortunately, Quicken is much more than an electronic record-keeper. It comes loaded with features that help you analyze your income and spending patterns, calculate your net worth, and plan to meet future goals. Although this book concentrates on Quicken's online capabilities, in this chapter we'll survey some of its most powerful tools for building your nest egg. These include:

- Generating informative financial reports
- Displaying graphs for a visual overview of key elements of your net worth
- Monitoring your financial status at a glance with snapshots and the progress bar
- Budgeting for future income and spending
- Setting up savings goals and financial forecasts
- Planning for retirement

NOTE

If you have the CD-ROM version of Quicken, you have access to a wealth of advice on how to save and make more money. *Finance 101* is a primer on personal finance with a twist: it will analyze your Quicken accounts to give you individualized guidance on investments, tax planning, and many other topics. *Ask the Experts* is an interactive multimedia application featuring prominent financial advisers Marshall Loeb and Jane Bryant Quinn. In short animated talks, they offer tips on key subjects bearing on your personal financial circumstances (of course, you need a sound card to hear what they say). To get the most from these programs, fill in Quicken's Personal Profile by opening the Deluxe Gateway (see Chapter 2) and clicking **Personal Profile** on the Gateway screen.

Generating Reports for Fast Financial Analysis

No matter how accurate and detailed your financial records, they're not very useful for managing and planning your finances until you organize them into an easily understandable form. Fortunately, Quicken comes with a reporting system that makes it a snap to generate financial reports that analyze your records from a variety of perspectives.

The quickest way to display a report is to click the **Reports** button on the iconbar:

You'll see the Create Report window (Figure 10.1), offering easy access to all of Quicken's reports. As you can see, the window is organized into six tabbed sections corresponding to various groupings of Quicken reports. Click a tab to display the associated panel and the reports available in that group.

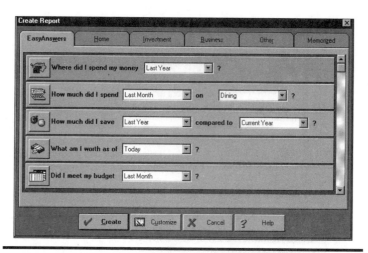

Figure 10.1 Build reports starting with the Create Report window.

Fast Reports with Quicken's EasyAnswers

The simplest way to display a report is to use the first tabbed panel, labeled **EasyAnswers**. As shown in Figure 10.1, the EasyAnswers panel lets you generate a report by picking a question you want to answer about your finances. For example, the first question is "Where did I spend my money?"

Before generating the report, complete the question by selecting the time period you want the report to cover—use the drop-down list (a quick tip: *Don't choose "last year" unless you were using Quicken to record transactions then*). Then click the large button beside the question. You'll get a category-by-category listing of your total earnings and spending for the period, something like the one shown in Figure 10.2. This report is based only on your Quicken "bank" accounts, omitting transactions from other account types.

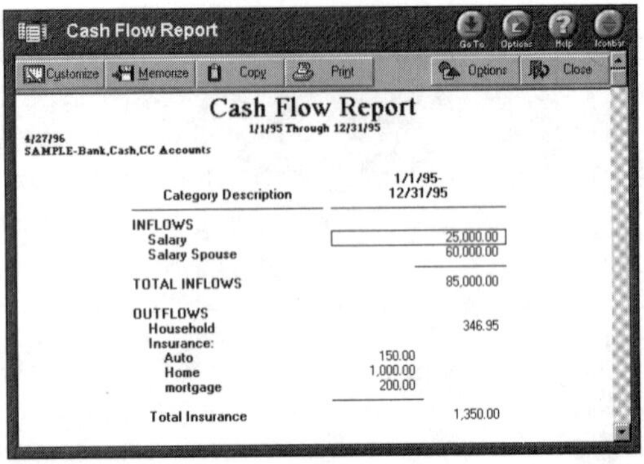

Figure 10.2 An example of a report you generated by choosing the first option on the EasyAnswers panel.

The question answered by the second option begins "How much did I spend?" Your job is to pick choices from the two drop down lists, one for the time period you want to analyze, the second for the category you want to study (if you want a comprehensive report, select **Everything** in the second drop-down list). When you click the button for this option, the report you'll generate details each and every transaction in the period, grouped by categories. Transactions from all your accounts are included.

The other options in the EasyAnswers panel work in like fashion but generate different types of reports. Because Quicken presents the questions to be answered by each report in plain English, it's easy to decide which report you should generate to get the information you want. There are more options than will fit in the window, so use the scroll bar at the right to view the remaining options.

You'll learn about creating other types of Quicken reports shortly. First, though, let's see how to work with Quicken reports on the screen.

Working with Reports on the Screen

The main part of the report window contains the report itself. If the entire report doesn't fit in the window you can move to see other portions using the scroll bars along the bottom and right side. In some reports, small diamonds with protruding vertical lines separate the column headings. You can drag these shapes with the mouse to change the column width.

Every report has a toolbar with buttons for common actions. The buttons and their functions are as follows:

- *Customize*—Lets you tailor the information shown in the report to your specific analysis objective. We'll cover customizing reports in more detail later in this chapter.

- *Memorize*—Records the report definition so you can generate the same report again later. Use this button after you've prepared a customized report so you don't have to repeat your work. You can reuse a memorized report at any time by clicking the **Memorized** tab in the Create Report window and selecting the report you wish to see again.

- *Copy*—Copies the report to the Windows clipboard, from which you can paste it into documents in other programs such as a word processor or spreadsheet.

- *Sort*—This button appears only in itemized categories reports. It displays a list of sorting options for the transaction items listed in the report.

- *Print*—Prints the report, or saves it as a file on disk. The dialog box that appears when you click this button (Figure 10.3) lets you select fonts for the report headings and body and lets you see a preview of the report on your screen before you actually print it.

- *Options*—Displays a window that lets you select options for all your reports, not just the current one.

- *Close*—Closes the current report window.

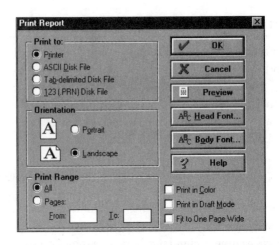

Figure 10.3 Use this dialog box to set options for your printed report, and to see a preview on the screen.

Using QuickZoom to See Report Detail

To see more detail about any line on a Quicken report, use QuickZoom. In most reports, when you move the mouse pointer over a dollar amount, the pointer becomes a magnifying glass with a Z in the center.

Double-clicking with this QuickZoom pointer produces a new report showing all the transactions that made up the total you clicked on. If you want to see more detail about an individual transaction, you can use QuickZoom on this new report, too. Double-clicking on the amount for any transaction takes you straight to that transaction in the account register (or, in the case of investment transactions, to the investment form showing the transaction details).

Types of Reports

The reports you generate from the EasyAnswers tab are each examples of one of Quicken's available report types. Once you're familiar with Quicken reports, or if you need a report type not offered on EasyAnswers, you can use the other tabbed panels in Create Reports to generate any report you need.

Quicken arranges the available report types into four groups, *Home, Business, Investment,* and *"Other,"* each with its own tab in the Create Reports window. On each of these panels, the individual reports are each listed with a brief description of the report's purpose and a small mockup of its layout (see Figure 10.4).

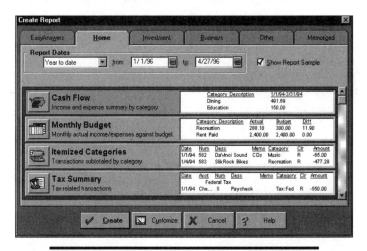

Figure 10.4 The Home tab in the Create Reports window shows these report choices.

As on the EasyAnswers panel, these panels contain more reports than will fit in the window. Use the scroll bar to see the remaining report types.

The **Home** panel offers the following reports:

- *Cash Flow* reports show total income and spending for each category over a specified period. They typically summarize the transactions from bank, cash, and credit card accounts.

- *Monthly Budget* reports compare the amount you've received or spent in each category with the amount you've budgeted. Bank, cash, and credit card accounts are included.

- *Itemized Categories* is the option for reports that list individually all the transactions from your account, grouped and subtotaled by category.

- *Tax Summary* reports show transaction-level detail like itemized category reports, but only for tax-related categories.

- *Net Worth* reports calculate your net worth by summarizing the balances from all your accounts on a given date.

- *Tax Schedule* reports list only the transactions you've assigned to categories associated with specific tax schedule line items, grouping the transactions by line item within each schedule.

- *Missing Checks* reports list all the checks in your register in order, indicating where breaks in the check number sequence have occurred.

- *Comparison reports* give you a category-by-category comparison of your income and spending over two time periods.

Click the **Investment** tab to access these reports:

- *Portfolio Value* reports generate information about individual investment holdings on a given date.

- *Investment Performance* reports show the annual return on your investments.

- *Capital Gains* reports summarize the actual gain or loss of investments that you purchased and then sold.

- *Investment Income* reports summarize the income your investments have generated from all sources, including dividends, interest, realized gains or losses, capital gains distributions, and if you like, unrealized "paper" gains or losses.

- *Investment Transactions* reports list the transactions recorded in your investment accounts, showing their impact on your cash balance and the value of your holdings.

The **Other** panel lists the five "generic" report types on which most other Quicken reports are based. Use them if you want to start a report from scratch without using the preset options chosen for you in the other report types. Here are the choices:

- *Transaction* reports detail individual transactions from one or more accounts. You decide which transactions should be listed and whether to group and subtotal them by category, class, payee, account, or time period.

- *Summary* reports present totals for categories, classes, payees, or accounts in the rows without listing individual transactions. If you like, you can break down these totals further into subtotals shown in columns according to time period, category, class, or account.

- *Comparison* reports compare amounts for a category, class, or account over two time periods in side-by-side columns. You can subdivide the main columns to break out amounts for shorter periods within them.

- *Budget* reports compare income and spending recorded in your accounts against the amounts you budgeted over a specific time period on a category-by-category basis.

- *Account Balances* reports calculate the overall balance in any group of accounts at any one time.

The reports available on the Business tab are oriented to the needs of small business owners. Their use is beyond the scope of this book, but they work just like the other types of Quicken reports.

Customizing a Report

You can alter the settings for any Quicken report so that it displays just the information you want to focus on. There are two ways to *customize* a report:

- Before you generate the report initially, highlight the report type you're starting with in the Create Reports window and click the **Customize** button.

- After you've already displayed the report, click the **Customize** button on the report toolbar.

Either way, you'll see the Customize Report window for the report type you've selected. Figure 10.5 shows an example.

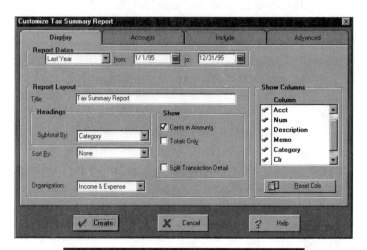

Figure 10.5 The Customize Report window.

The options in the Customize Report window are divided into a set of tabbed panels. Although the specific options vary a bit with the type of report, most of them are common to all report types:

- All the panels let you change the date or dates covered by the report.

- Use the *Display* panel to see the report title and its layout.

- In the *Accounts* panel, select the accounts you want to analyze in the report, individually or by type.

- The *Include* panel lets you pick the specific categories and classes covered in the report from lists, and lets you specify matching criteria that Quicken should use to select transactions for you (use the help system for information on setting up these matches).

- The *Advanced* panel lets you specify the types of transactions that appear in the report, exclude transactions below or above a dollar amount cutoff, and select transactions by their "cleared status," the entry in the Clr column in the register.

When you've finished making customization settings, click the **Create** button at the bottom of the Customize Report window to display the report.

Displaying Charts and Graphs

When you want an overview of the important trends in your financial life, graphs and charts are the best way to grasp the big picture. Graphs are a good complement for Quicken's reports. You can display a graph to get a visual idea, say, of your monthly income over the past year, and then generate a report to see the exact dollar amounts in specific income categories. Figure 10.6 shows a sample Quicken graph.

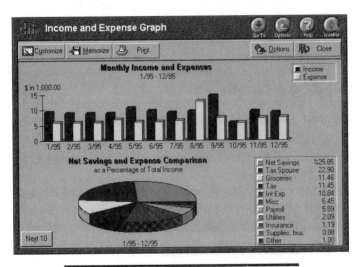

Figure 10.6 An Income and Expense graph.

To display a graph, open the Reports menu and choose **Graphs**. On the secondary menu, select the basic type of graph you want to work with.

Types of Quicken Graphs

Quicken offers four types of graphs:

- *Income and Expense* graphs show you the amount and sources of your income, as well as how much you're spending and what you're spending it on.

- *Budget Variance* graphs show how well you're meeting your budget targets month by month and category by category.

- *Net Worth* graphs give you a snapshot view of your overall net worth by comparing total assets against total liabilities. You can also get an idea of the relative contribution of each asset or liability to the totals.

- *Investment* graphs tell you how your total portfolio is divided among different securities or types of securities. You can also see how the prices and overall value of your investments have changed from month to month.

Displaying a Graph

Again, begin creating a graph by opening the Reports menu and choosing **Graphs** followed by the graph type you want. At this point you'll see a dialog box with options relevant to the type of graph you chose (Figure 10.7).

For all graph types, the three buttons at the bottom of the box let you select which accounts, categories, or classes Quicken includes in the calculations the graph represents. For Income and Expense and Budget Variance graphs, the checkbox labeled **Show Subcategories in Graph** is available. Check this box if you want to graph subcategories separately rather than lumping them in with the categories they belong to. A second checkbox, **Graph Supercategory Budgets**, appears only if you've selected a Budget Variance graph. Check this box if you want the graph to show supercategories.

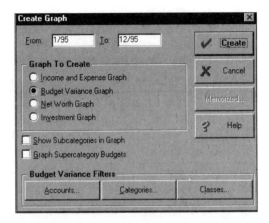

Figure 10.7 The Create Graph dialog box. Although you'll use the same box for all graphs, the options in the lower portion of the dialog box vary with the type of report you've chosen.

233

Inspecting Graph Details with QuickZoom

The four basic Quicken graph types are informative in themselves, but they also serve as gateways to a whole range of detailed information. Whenever you want to know more about almost any part of a graph, you just point to the item in question, click the mouse a time or two, and you'll have your answer.

When you move the mouse over a portion of the graph that you can analyze further, the mouse pointer becomes a magnifying glass with a Z in it, just as when you use QuickZoom in reports. Double-clicking with this magnifying glass pointer brings up a subsidiary graph or report with details on the item you're "inspecting."

For example, say you use QuickZoom in an Income and Expense graph. When you double-click with the QuickZoom pointer over a bar representing total income for a given month, you'll see a pie chart giving you a breakdown of the income total by category. If you now double-click over one of the pie slices, you'll see a report listing all the transactions for that category.

TIP

To see the dollar amount of any graph item such as a bar or pie slice, point to the item with the QuickZoom magnifying glass pointer and hold the mouse button down. The dollar amount appears in a small rectangle.

Financial Highlights at a Glance: Using Snapshots and the Progress Bar

If you want to monitor certain types of financial information on a regular basis, you can display it in a compact, visually compelling form with two Quicken features: *snapshots* and the *progress bar*:

- Snapshots are graphs or mini-reports illustrating information of your choice. Two or more snapshots appear on a single "page" of the Snapshots window, and you can create as many of these pages as you like.

- The progress bar appears at the bottom of the Quicken if you turn it on, showing two of several available summary statistics in graphical form. It lets you keep a constant watch on important indicators of your financial health.

Displaying Snapshots

To display the Snapshots window, open the Reports menu and click **Snapshots**. You'll see a window like the one shown in Figure 10.8, divided into areas that each contain a separate snapshot.

To substitute other snapshots for the ones already displayed, or to create a new snapshot page, click the **Customize** button on the toolbar. In the Customize Snapshots dialog box (Figure 10.9), begin by selecting the snapshot you want to change using the tiny mockup of the window in the upper left. After you pick a new snapshot from the list, you can customize its appearance and the information it contains with the controls on the right side of the box.

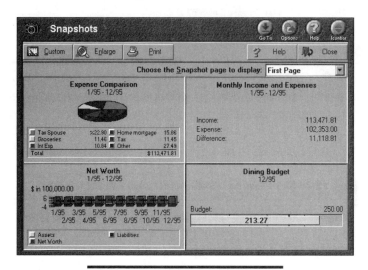

Figure 10.8 The Snapshots window.

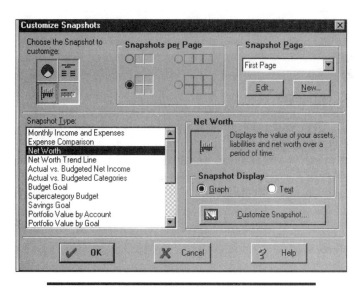

Figure 10.9 The Customize Snapshots dialog box.

235

To create a new snapshot page, click **New** at the upper right and type in a name. You choose which of the available pages Quicken displays with the drop-down list in the same area.

Working with Snapshots

Double-click over a snapshot to display it in larger form with more details (in some cases Quicken displays a related report instead). You'll get the same response if you click once to highlight the chosen snapshot, then click the **Enlarge** button on the toolbar. You can print out the snapshot by clicking the **Print** button.

Using the Progress Bar

The progress bar, shown in Figure 10.10, has room for only two gauges, but each measures your progress toward a vital budget target or savings goal. Besides, the progress gauge is small enough to remain on your screen while you use Quicken, allowing you to monitor these aspects of your financial situation on a continuous basis.

Figure 10.10 The progress bar.

Display the progress bar by opening the Plan menu and choosing **Progress Bar**. Each graph indicates your progress toward a specific goal as a bar extending horizontally from left to right. The red tick marks indicate graphically the goal you've set; the goal's dollar value appears at the right of the gauge. If the bar extends farther to the right than the red marks, you've overshot the goal (good for a savings goal, bad for a budget spending target). The progress bar appears green if you've got a comfortable cushion between your spending and your budget goal. It turns yellow as you approach the goal, and red if you overshoot it.

To choose the items displayed on the progress bar, click the icon labeled **Cust** at the far right of the bar. In the small box that appears (Figure 10.11), use the two drop-down lists to pick the gauge you want to display on both the left and right parts of the bar.

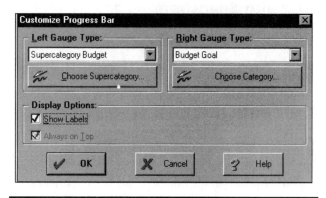

Figure 10.11 Use this box to customize the progress bar.

Your choices are:

- *Savings Goal*, to track how much money you've saved on your way to specific savings target.

- *Budget Goal*, to monitor how well you're keeping to budget in a chosen category.

- *Supercategory Budget*, to track your success in meeting your budget goal for an entire supercategory.

NOTE

Obviously, you must set up the budget targets and savings goals you want to monitor before you can use them in the progress bar.

After selecting the gauge type, click the correspondingly labeled button below to pick out the specific item you want to monitor.

Budgeting with Quicken

Budgeting is the quintessential financial management task. Quicken includes a built-in Budget worksheet that lets you prepare a detailed budget for all 12 months of the year. After a month or more has passed, you can use Quicken's budget reports and graphs to see how well you're holding to your budget in every category.

Preparing to Budget

Drawing up a formal budget can help you achieve your financial goals. A specific budget plan implies an important psychological commitment to spending discipline, and it turns vague notions about spending less into clear-cut dollar limits on every category.

Before you create a specific budget plan, however, you need a clear idea of your financial goals. Decide as clearly as you can what you want to accomplish: to pay off debts, save for a down payment, or set aside an emergency fund. Once you have a good sense of your goals, Quicken can help with the mechanics of the budgeting process, and with reports and graphs that provide the information you'll need to budget accurately.

Prepare for budgeting in Quicken by setting up all the accounts you need to accurately mirror your family's financial situation. Also, be sure your Quicken category list corresponds to your income and spending patterns. When the category list is ready, print it out as a paper scratch pad during the budgeting process (press **Ctrl-C** to display the list, then click **Print** to make a paper copy).

Creating a Quicken Budget

Quicken's budget worksheet is a great alternative to budgeting on paper. After you've completed the worksheet, Quicken uses it to create budget reports and graphs by comparing your actual income and spending to your budgeted projections.

When you first start working with Quicken, you'll have to use your paper records as the basis for your budget. Once you've entered your actual financial records for a month or more, you'll be able to use Quicken's automatic budgeting capability to extract your average income and spending in each category.

To build a Quicken budget, open the Plan menu and choose **Budgeting**. As shown in Figure 10.12, you'll be presented with the Budget window. This window is organized as a large table, similar to an accounting or computerized spreadsheet.

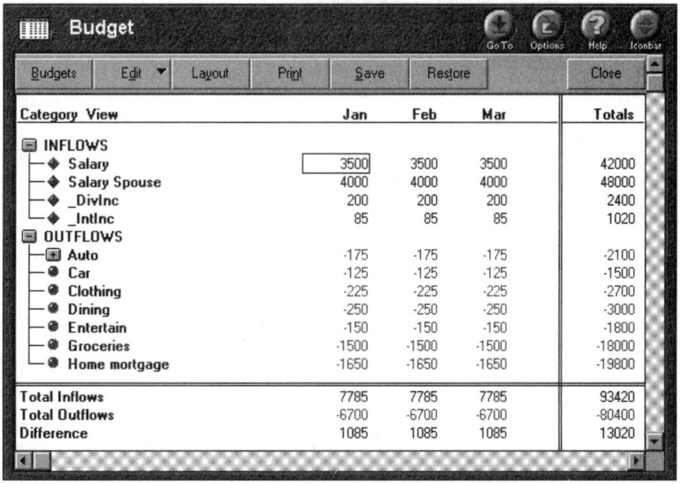

Category View	Jan	Feb	Mar	Totals
INFLOWS				
Salary	3500	3500	3500	42000
Salary Spouse	4000	4000	4000	48000
_DivInc	200	200	200	2400
_IntInc	85	85	85	1020
OUTFLOWS				
Auto	-175	-175	-175	-2100
Car	-125	-125	-125	-1500
Clothing	-225	-225	-225	-2700
Dining	-250	-250	-250	-3000
Entertain	-150	-150	-150	-1800
Groceries	-1500	-1500	-1500	-18000
Home mortgage	-1650	-1650	-1650	-19800
Total Inflows	7785	7785	7785	93420
Total Outflows	-6700	-6700	-6700	-80400
Difference	1085	1085	1085	13020

Figure 10.12 The Budget window.

In the rows of this table, the window lists all your Quicken categories in alphabetical order within two broad groups: *Inflows*, for income transactions, and *Outflows*, for expenses. The columns are the months of the year, though you can set up the screen so that columns correspond to quarters or entire years if you like.

The table lists budget items in outline form. At the top of the hierarchy are the two main groups, inflows and outflows. Individual categories are listed beneath them, with subcategories as the furthest branches out on the outline "tree." The table shows a box (instead of a green diamond or red dot) beside items having subsidiary branches of the outline beneath them. Click on the box to alternately hide or display these subsidiary branches.

NOTE

> You can display an additional outline level, grouping categories in their supercategories: click the **Layout** button and check the **Show Supercategories** box. Just be aware that if you make this choice, subcategories are listed on the same level as categories.

A thin selection rectangle marks the item that's currently selected for editing in the table. You can move the selection rectangle around the window with the cursor keys or the mouse.

Entering Budget Amounts

Type all the budget amounts for January in the first column of the table. With the selection rectangle still in the January column, copy the amounts to the remaining months by clicking the **Edit** button, then choosing **Fill Columns** from the menu that drops down. To enter a different amount for a category in a given month, just move the selection rectangle to the column for that month and type in the new amount.

As you fill in the table, your bottom-line objective is simple: you must keep your expenses lower than your income. After entering your projected monthly income from each source, focus on your expenses. Start by recording your *fixed expenses* (the ones you can't readily change), such as your mortgage payment or rent, car payment, other bank loans, your taxes, and your minimum utility bills. If you want to be disciplined about saving, you should include in your fixed expenses a minimum contribution to your savings or retirement account that you make without fail every month.

The moment of truth comes when you've finished entering your fixed expenses. Down at the bottom of the worksheet, Quicken has subtracted the total from your total income. What's left over—the amount labeled *Difference*—is available for your remaining expenses, your "discretionary spending."

Should this figure indicate you don't make enough money to sustain your current discretionary spending habits, you've just identified the reason that your savings account balance has been shrinking. The next, painful step is to adjust downward the limit for at least some of the discretionary spending items. You must make trade-offs between new clothes and nights out, between gourmet meals and an occasional vacation, until your income exceeds your total expenses. If that doesn't do the trick, you'll have to consider reducing your fixed expenses, perhaps by looking for a cheaper home or apartment, or trading in your car for a cheaper model. Or you may decide instead to search for ways to supplement your income.

Creating a Budget Automatically

Quicken can set up a budget for you based on the amounts you've actually recorded in your accounts for each category. Of course, you're free to go in and change any of the amounts you like after the automatic budget is established.

Here are the steps for setting up a budget automatically:

1. From the budget window, click the **Budgets** button on the toolbar. You'll see a window that lists all the budgets you've created (Figure 10.13).

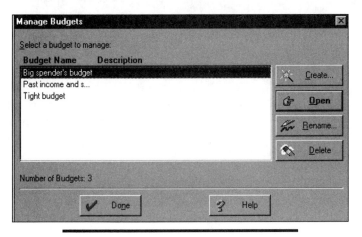

Figure 10.13 The Manage Budgets window.

2. Click **Create** to display a secondary box (Figure 10.14).

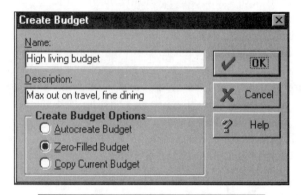

Figure 10.14 The Create Budget window.

3. Enter a name and description for your new budget. If it's not already selected, click the button labeled **Autocreate Budget**. Quicken displays a special window that lets you control how the automatic budget gets generated (Figure 10.15).

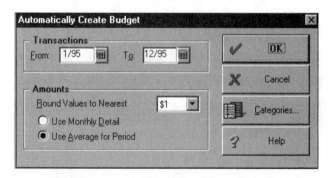

Figure 10.15 Use this window to set options for the budget Quicken generates automatically.

4. In the first two fields, enter the date range on which you want Quicken to base its automatic budget.

5. The Round Values to Nearest field lets you tell Quicken how to round off each category's monthly average: to the nearest $1, $10, or $100. Most of us who need to budget have to watch even small amounts, so the $1 option is a good choice.

6. Indicate the type of budget calculation you want Quicken to make. Click **Use Monthly Detail** if you want to transfer the actual category totals for each month to the worksheet; select **Use Average for Period** if you want Quicken to enter the average monthly amount for each category over the selected period.

7. To limit the automatic budget to specific categories, click **Categories**. In the list of your categories that appears, mark those you want Quicken to include in its budget calculations.

8. Click **OK** to generate the Automatic Budget.

Using Budget Reports

Two types of Quicken reports can help you plan your budget and see how well you're keeping to your earning and spending plans.

Itemized categories reports can be useful when you're designing your budget. They list all the transactions in your accounts organized by category and can be useful in drawing up a budget by helping you to analyze your spending in each category. If you think your total spending for say, clothing over the past couple of months, could have been trimmed, you can examine all your clothing purchases in the report and decide whether each purchase was necessary or a splurge.

To create an itemized categories report, select the **Home** tab in the Create Reports window and click the **Itemized Categories** button.

After you've kept track of all your income and expenses in Quicken for several months, use a *budget report* to see whether you've been able to keep to your budget. Select the **EasyAnswers** tab in the Create Report window if it isn't already visible. The last item is labeled "*Did I meet my budget?*" Here, select the time period you want to report on from the drop-down list, then click the button for this report. You'll get a report like the one shown in Figure 10.16, listing actual and budgeted amounts and the difference between them in three separate columns for each month.

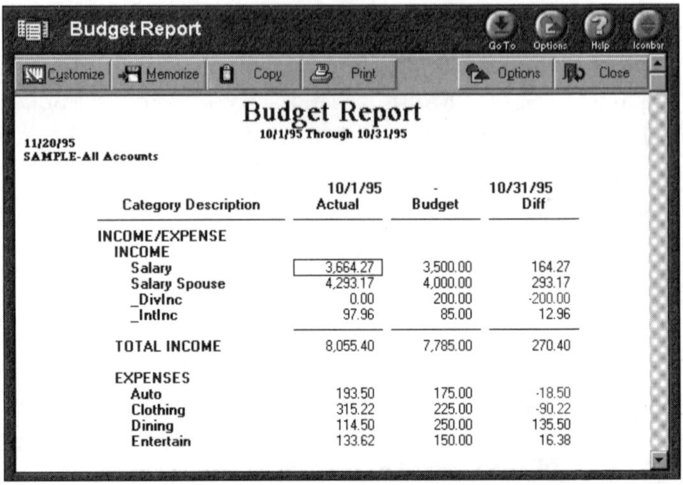

Budget Report
10/1/95 Through 10/31/95

11/20/95
SAMPLE-All Accounts

Category Description	10/1/95 Actual	- Budget	10/31/95 Diff
INCOME/EXPENSE			
INCOME			
Salary	3,664.27	3,500.00	164.27
Salary Spouse	4,293.17	4,000.00	293.17
_DivInc	0.00	200.00	-200.00
_IntInc	97.96	85.00	12.96
TOTAL INCOME	8,055.40	7,785.00	270.40
EXPENSES			
Auto	193.50	175.00	-18.50
Clothing	315.22	225.00	-90.22
Dining	114.50	250.00	135.50
Entertain	133.62	150.00	16.38

Figure 10.16 A sample Quicken budget report.

Getting the Big Picture with the Progress Bar and Budget Graphs

The quickest way to identify where you're spending too much money is to generate a Budget graph. The main graph covers the entire period you select, showing you at a glance the categories in which spending has most exceeded the budgeted amount. To see a month-by-month breakdown of your budgetary success (or failure) for any category, use QuickZoom on that part of the graph.

To keep an ongoing watch on how you well you're meeting budget targets, keep the progress bar on your screen set to show the supercategories or categories you need to monitor most closely. The progress bar is covered earlier in this chapter.

Basic Financial Planning

Quicken is loaded with features that make financial planning easier and more accurate. Reports and graphs can clarify your income and spending patterns, showing you quickly where you're spending too much money and allowing you to anticipate future income needs. But the most powerful Quicken tool for financial planning is its *forecasting* feature.

Of course, the quality of Quicken's forecasts depends on how much information you give it to work with. When you're first starting out with Quicken, you'll get accurate results only if you enter all your actual transactions from the past year or more. Otherwise, you'll have to rely on your own estimates of income and spending that may or may not correspond to reality.

Setting Savings Goals

245

One easy step you can take is to clarify your highest-priority financial objectives. Quicken lets you set up *savings goals* for this purpose. To define savings goals, open the Plan menu and click **Savings Goals**. The Savings Goals window is shown in Figure 10.17.

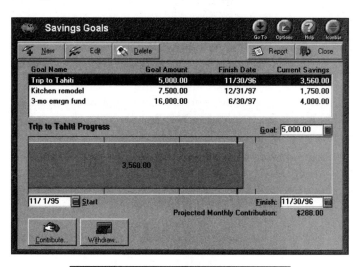

Figure 10.17 The Savings Goals window.

Once you've set up a savings goal, Quicken lets you "transfer" money from a regular bank account to a special account for the goal. Actually, the money remains in your real bank account, but you'll no longer have access to it in Quicken. That way, it's harder to spend on anything else.

To create a savings goal, click **New** in the Savings Goal window. Type in a name for the goal, the amount you want to save, and the target date for meeting your goal. Once you start transferring money into the savings goal account, Quicken will display your progress toward the goal in the lower part of the window (if you have two or more goals, click on the goal of interest in the upper part of the window).

NOTE

You can continuously monitor your progress toward a savings goal by displaying the progress bar, described later in this chapter.

"Contribute" to a savings goal by clicking the **Contribute** button at the lower right of the window. Quicken displays a window in which you can enter the amount of the contribution and select the account the funds will come from. If it turns out you need the money for other purposes, click the **Withdraw** button to transfer it back to the regular account.

Forecasting with Quicken

Quicken's forecasting feature predicts future earnings and spending based on transactions you've scheduled (see Chapter 6) as well as your past records. You can use Quicken forecasts to discover how soon you can afford a purchase, to plan spending and savings, and to find out what would happen to your finances if you took a new job, refinanced your mortgage, or made some other significant change in your earning or spending pattern.

To work with forecasts, open the Plan menu and choose **Forecasting**. The main portion of the Forecasting window, shown in Figure 10.18, shows a line graph of your account balances, showing the change in your bottom line over time.

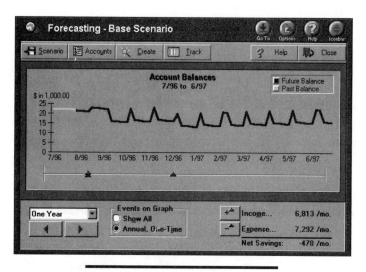

Figure 10.18 The forecast window.

The forecast for future account balances is shown in blue for positive values and red for negative, while all past balances appear in yellow. Individual items used to calculate the forecast are displayed as green and red triangles below the graph; clicking on one of these triangles lets you display the item details. When you first open the forecast window, the only items you'll see represent scheduled transactions that are due to be recorded in your account. You can add hypothetical items for purposes of forecasting only later.

Choosing Accounts to Display on the Forecasting Graph

Initially the forecasting graph reflects the combined balances of all your bank, credit card, cash, and savings goal accounts. This is generally the most useful selection, because it shows you how much "liquid" cash you'll have to save, invest, or spend, allowing you to plan accordingly. If you want to track your overall net worth, you need to graph all your accounts. On the other hand, you can restrict the graph to a single account to see how its balance will likely change over time.

To select the accounts that will appear on the graph, click the **Accounts** button in the toolbar. Choose the accounts you want from the list that appears and click **OK** to complete the task.

Creating Forecasts

You can base your forecasts on a variety of information sources: actual transactions already recorded in your account, scheduled transactions, income and expense items that you create for forecasting purposes only, and information from your Quicken budget. Because you can create as many different forecasts as you like, it's easy to compare the effect of varying your forecasting assumptions on your bottom line.

To create a forecast, start by assigning it a name. Click the **Scenario** button on the toolbar, then click **New**, and type in a name for this particular forecast. From now on, any changes you make to this "scenario" (meaning *named forecast*) will be saved until you create a new scenario. After you switch scenarios, you can go back to see any previous scenario the way it last appeared by clicking **Scenario** and choosing its name in the drop-down list.

Once the new scenario has a name, click the **Create** button on the toolbar. In the small window that appears, set the date range you Quicken to base the forecast on. When building the forecast, Quicken analyzes transactions in your accounts, scheduled transactions, or both that fall within this range.

Then click **Advanced** to tell Quicken what type of information to include in the forecast. At the top left, choose **Known Items** if you want to base the forecast only on transactions scheduled for entry in the period; **Estimated Items**, if you want Quicken to generate the forecast from your existing records or from your Quicken budget; or **Create Both** if you want to use both of these methods.

Next, if you chose either **Estimated Items** or **Create Both**, you must tell Quicken how to make its estimate. Choose **From Register Data** if you want to average the per-category amounts of the transactions already recorded in your accounts, or **From Budget Data** to use the amounts in your monthly budget (you must set up a budget first, of course).

Click **Done**, then **OK** to display the new forecast in the window. If you like, you can now adjust Quicken's calculations to match any changes you expect in your future financial circumstances. To change the amount of an item used to calculate the forecast, use the **Income** or **Expense** buttons at the bottom of the window.

As shown in Figure 10.19, either button displays a list of the items already included in your forecast. You can change the amount for any item by typing in a new amount, or make other changes by highlighting the item and clicking **Edit** or **Delete**. Click **Done** when you're through making changes.

249

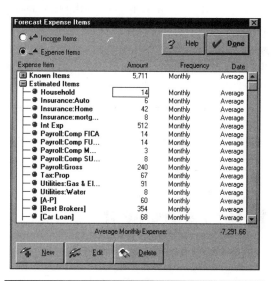

Figure 10.19 Make changes to the items used in Quicken's forecasting calculations in this window.

Adding Items to the Forecast

Quicken forecasts let you explore the repercussions on your financial future of every income or spending decision you might make. One way to "change the future" is to alter your budget and generate a new forecast based on the modified budget figures. But an even more powerful key to building hypothetical scenarios is to schedule transactions for forecasting purposes only. Quicken doesn't record these items in your accounts, but it includes them in the forecasting calculations and graph.

Let's say you're trying to decide whether to buy a new car or stick with your old clunker for another year. First, create a scenario that projects your account balances under current conditions. Now create a new scenario using the techniques described above, naming it something like "New car." Using the hypothetical forecasting items, you would now enter a one-time expense item for the new car's down payment and an item that recurs each month for the monthly payments. You'll immediately be able to see on the forecasting graph the impact of those expenses on your future account balances.

To add new forecasting items, click the **Income** button or the **Expense** button as appropriate. Click **New** to bring up a secondary window where you can enter the item details.

TIP

You can add new forecasting items more quickly by clicking the thin gray line below the graph. This displays the New Item window directly.

Planning for Retirement

Eventually you'll reach the stage of life where you no longer want to work, at least not in a regular, full-time job. With Quicken's retirement calculator, you can easily answer the all-important retirement-planning question: How much money do I have to put aside each year for an adequate nest egg?

WARNING

Although the retirement calculator gives results down to the penny, don't be fooled: Its projections are only rough estimates based on a number of inevitably inaccurate assumptions you must make. Still, it's a great way to test alternative hypothetical scenarios.

To use the retirement calculator, choose **Financial Planners and Retirement** from the Activities menu. Figure 10.20 shows what you'll see. The retirement calculator is the largest of Quicken's calculators on the screen, with a good many fields to fill out. But don't worry—it's really quite straightforward.

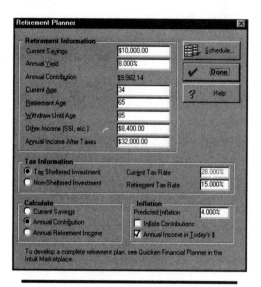

Figure 10.20 The retirement calculator.

You can use the retirement calculator to figure three kinds of results, depending on what you want to know. Select one of the radio buttons at the bottom left of the window to tell Quicken which result to calculate:

- *Current Savings* if you want to know how much money you'll have to place in your retirement account now to reach your yearly retirement income goal.

- *Annual Contribution* if you want to know how much you must add to your retirement fund each year.

- *Annual Retirement Income* if you want to know what your yearly income will be, based on how money you plan to set aside.

Notice that when you select a radio button, Quicken eliminates the corresponding field, placing a calculated value that you can't change in its place.

NOTE

Fill out the remaining fields with your best estimates of their correct values as follows.

If you haven't asked Quicken to calculate the Current Savings fields, enter the equivalent cash value of any investments you've earmarked for your retirement fund (not the total in your savings account). If you did ask Quicken to calculate this field, the result tells how much "seed money" you must put into this fund when you open it, based on your other entries.

In the Annual Yield field, try to be conservative about estimating your yearly return on your retirement accounts and investments.

Type the amount you expect to contribute to your retirement fund each year in the Annual Contribution field. You'll then be able to see how much retirement income a given yearly contribution will produce. You can set Quicken to calculate this value if you want to see how much you must set aside each year to meet an income target.

You don't have to enter your actual age in the Current Age field. If your finances are limited at the moment, and you don't think you can put aside money for retirement yet, you can see how the age at which you start your retirement fund affects how much you must contribute, or how much retirement income you'll have.

Vary the entry in the Retirement Age field if you'd like to see how this affects the yearly contribution required to meet an income goal, or your expected retirement income with a given annual contribution. Since you can't predict your longevity, the Withdraw Until Age field has to be a complete guess, but it also influences your results in dramatic ways.

In the Other Income field, enter the yearly amount you expect to receive from any other sources, including social security, pensions, and so on, during your retirement.

The amount in the Annual Income After Taxes field is the critical determinant of your retirement standard of living. If you've asked Quicken to calculate the result, the value displayed is based on your entries in other fields. Otherwise, type in how much income you want when you retire. Keep in mind that this field can be set to show either the actual number of dollars you can expect to receive annually, or your spending power in today's dollars, depending on whether you've checked the **Annual Income in Today's $** box.

Select the **Tax Sheltered Investment** radio button if your retirement savings won't be taxed until you withdraw them; otherwise select **Nonsheltered Investment**. If you have a mixture of taxable and tax-sheltered retirement investments, you should prepare separate calculations for each type, and then add the totals.

Fill in the Retirement Tax Rate with your best guess of what your overall income tax rate will be when you retire. Unfortunately, given the vagaries of politics and tax policy, this value is impossible to predict, but it has a major impact on the calculations you make.

253

If your retirement investments are tax-sheltered, you must enter your Current Tax Rate. Although your current rate should be easier to estimate, remember that the calculations you make are based on the unlikely assumption that this rate will stay constant throughout your working life. For the most accurate results the rates you enter in both fields should be those of your overall income tax bracket, including both state and federal taxes.

Finally, handle the three inflation-related fields at the lower right of the window, as follows. Make your best estimate of the average rate of inflation in the Predicted Inflation field. Given the track record of many "leading economists," your own guess may be as good as anyone's—but again, your results depend very heavily on the number you enter here.

If you check the **Inflate Contributions** box, the calculator assumes you'll be increasing your contribution to the retirement fund by the percentage inflation rate you predict. This is definitely the wisest course—assuming just a 4% yearly inflation rate, in 25 years a $2000 contribution will have the spending power of only about $500 today.

If you don't increase your contribution to keep pace with inflation, you'll have to make much larger contributions from the outset to meet a given goal.

Check the last box, **Annual Income in Today's $**, if you want the results shown in the Annual Income After Taxes field to reflect the buying power, adjusted for inflation, of your yearly retirement income—assuming that you withdraw the equivalent amount each year. If, for example, the Retirement Income field displays $20,000 when this box is checked, the amount you can withdraw each year after taxes will buy goods and services now worth $20,000. To see the actual amount you'll be able to withdraw each year, uncheck the box. This figure is interesting because it can get pretty large, but you shouldn't pay any real attention to it: since inflation rapidly erodes the value of a dollar, a figure that sounds like a lot of money may represent only modest purchasing power. Because of inflation, the amount you actually collect will increase each year, however the purchasing power remains constant.

Quicken recalculates the field you've selected each time you move the cursor from field to field. If you want to see the actual dollar amounts—adjusted for inflation—of your yearly contributions or withdrawals, click **Schedule** to pop up the Deposit Schedule window.

When you're through making retirement calculations, put the calculator away by choosing **Done**.

Keeping Track of Your Retirement Fund

To organize your retirement fund recordkeeping efficiently, establish a separate Quicken account for each component investment portfolio. In a simple scenario, you might have one account for your IRAs, and one for your mutual funds. Use investment accounts for all tax-deferred investments (including IRAs, 401(K) plans, and tax-sheltered annuities). That way, you can designate the accounts as tax-deferred when you set them up, and Quicken will exclude their earnings from tax reports. Track retirement funds you keep in non-tax-sheltered CDs or savings accounts in Quicken bank accounts. To

254

make these accounts easy to find, the name of each should begin with the same first few characters, as in "Ret-IRA," "Ret-Mut'l Funds," and so on.

When you make contributions to any of these accounts, transfer the money from your main bank account. Transfers to tax-deferred accounts will still appear on your tax reports, so you'll be able to deduct these amounts from your taxable income on your tax returns.

If your employer makes contributions to your IRA or 401(K) plan, enter these amounts in the same investment account you use to record your own contributions. Employer contributions require two transactions. First, account for the funds—enter **MiscInc** in the Action field, fill in the Amount field, and categorize the transaction as "EmployerIRA," "Employer 401," or what have you. Then enter a Buy transaction for the purchased "security" (whether it's stock or just a CD) in the same amount. The first transaction identifies the employer contribution, while the second adjusts the value of the particular investment.

255

When you receive interest payments on an IRA or similar savings plan, enter them as deposit transactions directly into the corresponding account. See Chapter 9 for instructions on keeping track of changes in the values of investments such as stocks, bonds, and mutual funds, and of dividends and other investment income.

You can use an Account Balances report to find the current value of all your retirement-related accounts. Customize the report, giving it an appropriate title, such as "Current Value of Retirement Fund." Leave the second date field set to today's date, and the Intervals field set to **None**. Then click the **Accounts** tab and select only your retirement accounts for inclusion in the report.

When the report appears on the screen, memorize it for future use. When you memorize it, leave the radio button labeled **None** selected in the Memorize Report window. This way, whenever you reuse the report it will automatically show you the value of your retirement holdings as of that day.

Monitoring Your Net Worth

Net worth is the amount of money you'd have if you sold everything you own and paid off all your debts. In accountant's terms, that's equivalent to the total value of all your liabilities subtracted from the total value of all your assets. Even though you aren't worth as much as you'd like, you're probably worth considerably more than you suspect—and Quicken can tell you just how much more with a few quick clicks of the mouse.

It can be an ego boost to know your net worth, but there are practical reasons to determine it as well. The security and comfort of your retirement depend heavily on your net worth, since you may need to sell some of your possessions to generate cash when you're no longer working. And by knowing what the value of your estate will be when you die, you'll be able to determine whether you'll be leaving enough to your survivors; if not, you can purchase more life insurance. In addition, you can estimate the tax bill your survivors will have to pay and plan accordingly.

Figuring your net worth in Quicken couldn't be easier, provided you set up all your accounts properly in the first place. Obviously, since your net worth reflects *all* your assets and *all* your liabilities, you must record them all in Quicken. That means you must set up Quicken asset accounts for assets that you don't see in monthly financial statements, such as jewelry, works of art, valuable furniture, and so on. You also need to set up paired asset and liability accounts for items such as your home or car in which you have equity but on which you still owe money. For such items, place the equity value in the asset account and the loan balance in the liability account (see Chapter 8 for details on accounting for loans with Quicken).

With all your assets and liabilities ensconced in accounts, calculating your net worth is simply a matter of producing a Net Worth report. Click the **Reports** button, switch to the EasyAnswers tab, and click the button for the choice, "What am I worth today?" If you want to calculate your net worth at another point in time, use the drop-down list to pick the date.

If you want to see your net worth graphically, generate a Net Worth graph by opening the Reports menu and clicking **Graphs —> Net Worth**. Click over the graph to display the dollar value of any portion. Figure 10.21 depicts a Net Worth graph. You can also monitor your net worth with a snapshot (snapshots are covered earlier in this chapter).

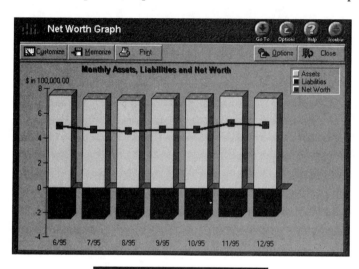

Figure 10.21 Net Worth graph.

Summary

By now, you're thoroughly familiar with how Quicken can help you analyze your past earnings and spending and plan for your financial future. Because you'll be able to keep complete records so easily with your online banking program, Quicken's reporting, budgeting, and forecasting tools become that much more powerful aids in the quest to build your net worth.

CHAPTER ELEVEN:

Finances on the Internet: Quicken and Beyond

With what seems like every business on the planet rushing to establish an online presence on the Internet, it's no surprise that Internet-based financial services are proliferating wildly. While Quicken's online resources will meet your basic banking and investment needs, there will soon be a cornucopia of new services on the Internet covering everything from basic banking to advanced investing and specialized financial research.

Quicken itself can serve as your gateway to all the Internet has to offer, including these financial services. Quicken Deluxe includes the software you need for free access to the Quicken Internet site, called the *Quicken Financial Network*. For a fee, you can upgrade to a full-blown Internet connection.

A Quick Internet Primer

Originally developed by governmental agencies and universities, the Internet is a network of computers spanning the globe. While the Internet has always been used for exchanging electronic mail and other information, it's the emergence of the World Wide Web that has driven the Internet's mushrooming popularity over the past two or three years.

The *World Wide Web* puts information on your screen in a graphical format like you're familiar with if you use Windows. Text, graphics, and even sound and animation are presented together, and you can jump from one topic to another without having to keep track of which computer on the network contains the information you're currently browsing.

Most home and small business users connect to the Internet over standard telephone lines using high-speed modems. It's also possible, and much faster, to use special telecommunications connection such as ISDN lines.

Using Quicken Financial Network

The Quicken Financial Network, or *QFN*, is an Internet site offered by Intuit, Quicken's publisher. So far—as of late 1995—QFN provides a relatively modest set of services. Already, though, you can find items of real value on QFN. And over the next year or so, Intuit plans to turn QFN into a leading online source for financial information and services.

If you don't already have a hookup to the Internet, you can connect to QFN from Quicken, as long as your modem is fast enough. The minimum modem speed for Internet access is 9600 bits per second (bps), though 14.4 kbps (kilobits per second) or 28.8 kbps modems are preferable.

Navigating the Internet also requires special software, but Quicken Deluxe comes with what you need: a limited version of *Netscape Navigator*, one of the most popular "browsers" for the World Wide Web. QFN access is free with this version of Netscape, but you can't connect to the rest of the Internet. If you're willing to pay for the privilege, you can register for full access to the Internet—including the Web, Internet electronic mail, and newsgroups—once you're connected to QFN.

Information and Services Available on QFN

Services now available on QFN include:

- *The NetWorth mutual fund advisory service.* Probably the most substantial service currently available on QFN, NetWorth lets you research the performance of mutual funds you own or are considering for purchase. In addition, you can participate in online discussions of financial trends and investment strategies with well-known financial advisors and managers of highly-rated mutual funds.

- *An online guide to Quicken.*

- *Detailed information on the online offerings of various financial institutions.*

- *Online communications with Intuit.* You can read messages from Intuit about future products and services and send your suggestions, compliments, or complaints.

- *Online shopping for Quicken supplies and other Intuit software.*

Connecting to QFN

Assuming you're new to the Internet and don't already have an Internet browser, here's how to connect to QFN:

1. Open the Online menu and click **Quicken Financial Advisor**.

2. You'll see a message box explaining some of the basics of how QFN works and asking if you want to register for the service. To see additional information about QFN and the Internet, click **More Info**. You'll return to this box when you've finished reading the information. When you're ready to register, click **Yes**.

3. Quicken next displays a message box with a disclaimer covering the terms of your access to the Internet. To indicate your agreement with the terms, click **Accept**.

4. The first Netscape Navigator window appears. Click **Continue** to proceed to the Netscape Registration Wizard window (Figure

261

11.1). Here, you'll proceed through the numbered buttons to enter your personal registration information, set up your modem, and connect to QFN.

5. Click **User Information**. In the next series of dialog boxes, enter your name, address, and phone number. Click **Done** when these are complete.

6. Back at the main Netscape Registration Wizard window, be sure your modem is ready and click **Modem Setup**. As you proceed through the dialog boxes, Quicken detects your modem and sets up the program accordingly. If Quicken can't detect the modem, you can enter the modem type and speed manually. Return to the Netscape Registration Wizard window.

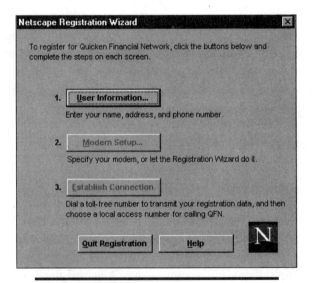

Figure 11.1 The Netscape Navigator Wizard.

7. Click **Establish Connection**. When the Netscape Navigator connects to QFN, you'll see a window like the one shown in Figure 11.2.

Figure 11.2 The QFN home page.

If You Already Use the Internet...

If you already have a Web browser and an Internet service provider, you have two choices for accessing QFN:

1. You can use your current browser, accessing QFN at the following address:

   ```
   http://www.intuit.com/
   ```

   Use this method if you pay a flat rate for unlimited Internet access.

2. You can use Quicken to access QFN and your other browser for the rest of the Internet. Since QFN access is free via Quicken, this method is better if you pay by the minute or hour for Internet access.

Other Financial Services on the Internet

At this writing, Internet-based financial services are poised to take off. Financial institutions, software companies, and hordes of independent entrepreneurs are racing to develop sophisticated online systems for distributing financial information and speeding financial transactions.

To date, however, relatively few of these services have been unveiled. But if you search for them, you can already find:

- real-time stock price quotes (without the 15 minute delay of Investor Insight quotes)
- online stock and commodity trading
- daily stock market reports
- financial advice columns and publications

Though limited in number, many of the services now available on the Web are free. Of course, you can expect this to change rapidly as public acceptance grows for online financial management.

Summary

Quicken itself provides everything you need for online banking, and plenty of online resources for investment as well. But there's a rapidly growing galaxy of other online financial services available via the World Wide Web, and you can now access them all through Quicken.

PPENDIX A

Online Banking Numbers

Online banking hotline: 800/224-1047

Call this number to hear an up-to-date list of financial institutions offering online banking via Quicken.

Intuit Services Corporation: 708/585-8500

Call this number to sign up for online bill payment if your financial institution isn't listed below (you can sign up for online bill payment with any financial institution).

Investor Insight/Portfolio Price Update: 800/245-2164

Gives recorded information about Quicken's online investment services.

American Express: 800/AXP-7500

Bank of Boston: 800/476-6262

Centura Bank: 800/721-0501

Chase Manhatten Bank: 800/CHASE24

Chemical Bank: 800/CHEMBANK

Citibank: 800/446-5331

Compass Bank: 800/COMPASS

CoreStates Bank: 800/562-6382

Crestar Bank: 800/CRESTAR

First Chicago: 800/800-8435

First Interstate Bank: 800/YOU AND I

Home Savings of America (Savings of America): 800/310-4932

M&T Bank: 800/790-9130

Marquette Banks/E Direct: 800/708-8870

Michigan National Bank: 800/CALL-MNB

Quicken Credit Card (Travelers Bank): 800/772-7889

Sanwa Bank: 800/23SANWA

Smith Barney: 800/221-3636

SunTrust Bank: 800/382-3232

Texas Commerce Bank: 800/235-8522

Union Bank: 800/796-5656

   Union Bank's Bank@Home program offers free online banking for the first 12 months and a $50 rebate on the purchase of Quicken.

U.S. Bank: 800/422-8762

Wells Fargo: 800/423-3362 extension Q

INDEX

Intuit Membership, 22, 26, 28, 68, 94

Investment accounts 148, 197, 200-202. *See also* Securities

adjusting share and cash values, 212

entering investment transactions in, 203-210

mutual funds, for, 201-202

Investment graphs, 232

Investment Income reports, 228

Investment Performance reports, 228

Investment reports, 228

Investment Transactions reports, 228

Investments. *See* Securities

Investor Insight, 180-200, 217-220

automated online connections, 187

charting security performance, 187

company reports, 194-195

financial news, 191-192

flash reports, 192

obtaining investment information with, 186-187

personal reports, 193-194

price histories, using in Quicken, 219

price reports, 193

Quicken, compared to, 200

signing up, 181-183

stock quotes, using in Quicken, 219-220

IRAs, 147, 171, 202, 254-255

Itemized Categories reports, 228

K
Keyboard shortcuts, 37

L
Liability accounts. 148, 170

Loans, tracking with Quicken, 170-178

amortized loans, 177-178

online repeating payments, paying with, 118, 173

scheduled transactions, paying with, 126

M
Macintosh, 3

Memorized reports, 225

Memorized Transaction List, 111-114

deleting, 112

memorized transactions, 109-114

locking and unlocking, 113-114

paying loans with, 176-177

using, 111

Menus, Quicken, 37

Missing Checks reports, 228

Modem, 3-4

requirements to run Quicken, 12

setting up

Investor Insight, for, 182

online banking, for, 24-25

Quicken Financial Network, for, 262

Money market funds, 152